Rise of the Personal Brand

Stories from entrepreneurs, influences, and digital marketers

Matt Bertram, Billy Bray, Chris Burres, Nolen Daivs, Mack Blankenship, Randall Chesnutt, Kailee Wong, Freddy Goerges, Taylor Waidhofer, Sami Khaleeq

Published by EWR Media

Copyright © 2020 by Matt Bertram

All rights reserved. This book or any portion thereof may not be reproduced or used in any manner whatsoever without the express written permission of the publisher except for the use of brief quotations in a book review or scholarly journal.

First Printing: 2020

ISBN: 979-8-57912-492-0

U.S. trade bookstores and wholesalers please contact:

EWR Media

(713) 592-6724

13105 Northwest Freeway Ste 765

Houston, Texas 77040

Ordering Information:

Special discounts are available on quantity purchases by corporations, associations, educators, and others. For details, contact the publisher at the above listed address.

Table of Contents

How Brands Connect with Matt Bertram — 1

How to Build A Memorable Online Brand with Chris Burres — 17

The Secrets of Selling with Billy Bray — 29

Your Network Determines Your Net Worth with Nolen Davis — 39

How to Create a Digital Footprint in the Mortgage industry with Mortgage Mack — 49

Build a Strong Foundation for Your Business with Randall Chesnutt — 60

Healthy Body, Healthy Mind with Kailee Wong — 89

How to Turn Adversity into Success with The LinkedIn Authority with Freddy Goerges — 103

Create Shock Value and Prove Your Naysayers Wrong with Taylor Waidhofer — 115

Growth Strategies to Scale your Business in the Digital Era with Sami Khaleeq — 12129Chapter Summaries — 135

Acknowledgements & Works Cited — 151

How Brands Connect with Matt Bertram

The more you share, the more you will sell.

Let me explain.

In the early 2000's, a global conversation began through technological innovation that every man and woman could participate in. Due to increased smartphone connectivity, instant communication, and ease of use of social sharing platforms, the ability to spread new ideas, news, products, and services can happen in the blink of an eye.

As you discover all the possibilities the internet provides, you can break boundaries and belief systems and leverage the benefits to grow your business! Now, even the smallest of businesses can achieve a global reach. One person with a smartphone can connect with millions and change the world.

At no other time in history has it been so easy for businesses to connect and engage with their ideal consumer.

Did you know that, on average, we check our phones over 100 times a day and emails over 30 times every hour?

Yet, you may still feel like the proverbial hamster on the wheel. You keep running faster and faster, but every day feels like a struggle to just keep your head above water. You may be thinking to yourself... *I've tried "social media marketing," but it didn't work. And it costs so much money!*

One possible reason for this is that most businesses don't fully understand the impact social media has on sales and revenue, or how to effectively navigate the social media waters to connect with their target audience. Instead, social media has turned into businesses promoting their products/services without actually providing any value. What many of these businesses don't realize is that you need to go back to the basics and be social on social media. Understanding this evolution of social media, and the users and brands all interacting with each other, is becoming increasingly sophisticated — and with sophistication often comes confusion. People, companies, and brands alike are expected to be more "human" on social media. That means engagement, communication, sharing, etc. Consumers on social media want to be treated as individuals, not demographics.

In this "new economy," adaptation is a critical skill. You must be able to see red flags from a mile away and take notice of shifting winds in the buyer's behavior, marketing, and communication. "The Cluetrain Manifesto," written over ten years ago, provided some influential and fairly accurate predictions. Here are some of the key takeaways:

- Markets are conversations and should be conducted in a human voice.
- These conversations are enabling new forms of social organization and knowledge exchange.
- As a result, markets are getting more knowledgeable, organized, and up-to-date with current events.

Today, more than ever, conscious consumers are overwhelmed with noisy content overload and expressing backlash in response. It is estimated that a shocking 2.5 quintillion bytes of data are created every single day--a completely unfathomable number! With growing skepticism and increased connectivity in the marketplace, there is an increased desire for transparency, authenticity, and trust. The answer to cutting through all this noise and connecting directly with your target audience lies in a concept called **"Mindful Brand Linking" (MBL)**. In my last best-selling book, "Build Your Brand Mania," I explain how individuals and businesses are brands, and that the recurring patterns those brands portray have been used by successful business owners over and over again. To further break it down for you, I will describe my 'MBL strategy' for you to see footprints in examples and stories shared by other influencers, entrepreneurs, and small business owners in the subsequent chapters.

Mindful Brand Linking focuses on the psychology of identification and mindfulness coupled together to create deep and powerful connections between you, your company, your brand, and your audience online. Scientific studies tell us that the need to belong, matter, and connect is hardwired into our human psyche.

Mindful

Let's break it down. The secret to success starts with intention. We all know that words and images have power. But, in reality, few people or businesses take the time to think deeply about the value, purpose, and 'why' of their brand. Most are just sharing to share.

Remember this--attention is currency. We value it. We do everything in our power to earn it. However, most fail to consider how much of it we waste in the process of gaining it. Self-expression has indeed become the main driver of social media, but is not self-reflection equally important? And since we are in the mindset of truly looking at what we are doing and being vulnerable about it with all this "mindfulness talk," do you believe small and medium-sized business brands are truly sharing based on self-expression? Every word, image, graphic, and video needs to be thoughtful.

Here are a few questions to help you get to know your target audience:

- When you share content on social media, are you aware of your target demographics, or *who* exactly you want to reach?
- Do you know their needs, wants, and desires?
- Are you answering questions? Solving problems, listening, responding, and being helpful?

- Does your product or service make your audience smile, laugh, and create experiences that are enjoyable, memorable, and shareable?

Mindful Marketing is about making connections and expressing empathy. It takes more than basic customer lip service to care and have your customer's best interest at heart genuinely. Consider taking a "walk in their shoes" to catch a glimpse into their lives. This helps you to understand the needs of your ideal customers better. Then, with this in mind, designing and offering products around those needs in a way that adds value to their lives is easy. This should translate into your content strategy on social media. Over time, this will become second nature. It will start the process of evangelism around your company, building customer loyalty, and converting fans into lifelong clients.

Mindfulness in Marketing means:

- Attention is a currency
- Acting with intention
- Connecting through empathy

Disney is an example of a brand that knows its customers inside and out. As a corporation, Disney strives to make its customers happy. One way they do this is by laying out the parks in a way that reduces lines for rides—creating a unique experience for their customers to enjoy. As you can see from their massive success year after year, mindfulness is at the core of Disney parks.

There are many benefits of incorporating mindfulness in marketing, both for the bottom line of your business and for your current and future customers. Finding new ways to attract customers through empathy and greater awareness is a powerful tool that helps you cut through the clutter and speak directly to your audience.

Lastly, it's important to give you a lens or framework from which all this should be shared or viewed. Think about what your relationship is to your audience. Are you a friend, teacher, or coach? Maybe a trusted advisor? At our agency, one metric we pay close attention to when we design a content strategy comes from Google's Quality Raters' Guidelines. It is a term called **Expertise, Authority, and Trustworthiness** (E.A.T). It is Google's attempt to simplify for human consumption all the algorithm's signals from the links, website layouts and user experience to explain what a person looks for when deciding to make a purchasing decision. To rise to the top in your industry, you must not only be an expert but also influential and trustworthy.

Brand

A person is a brand. A company is a brand. A brand is a person. Everything you do or don't do impacts your brand either negatively or positively. A contributor in this book always wears a bowie tie. In doing so, he brands himself as someone who is always dressed to the "9's". Tom's Shoe Company brands themselves as a compassionate company that betters the world one shoe sale at a time. Everything you do--the way you look, speak, feel, touch, and act creates your personal and professional brand.

Think of your brand as a living organism; let's take a plant, for example. Plants start out as a seed. Over time, they sprout out from the ground looking for sunlight. The DNA of the plant is akin to the nature of your brand essence. What will your brand look like once it's fully grown? Many companies skip this step of brand introspection, which ties very closely with mindfulness and being aware of who we are and what is going on around us. A close friend of mine calls this being "woke." I'm not sure that is the same definition the internet gives it, but you get the idea. Mainly, I see people jump straight to product planning and marketing tactics. The overall vision and business strategy are often left in the dust, which has had a detrimental effect on the marketing and customer journey experience as a whole.

Your Brand is Your Most Valuable Asset

So, why invest in branding? The operative word here is "investment." It's the most effective way to increase your marketing efforts over the long term. Branding is why people should choose you over your competitor. It enables you to attract better customers with lower marketing costs, and customers are happy to pay a little more for your offerings because of how it makes them feel. It creates a smoother sales process with a much higher conversion rate and stronger customer loyalty. Think about how much easier it is to close a referral. The person that is being referred has already bought into the idea that you're a high-quality brand due to your association with the person who referred them. At the end of the day, what could be a smarter investment for your company than investing in things that shape the way that the world perceives you or your company?

Brands are perceptions, and they live in the mind. How an individual perceives a brand, consciously or unconsciously, determines how they will engage with that brand. Perceptions are also malleable. In today's chaotic world, we are constantly searching for meaning and order. We tend to look for a "Trusted Advisor" to help us make sense of our realities. Without it, we're lost.

Branding has the power to shape reality. As far as our brains are concerned, there's no real difference between perception and reality. That is why dreams are so real. What we perceive to be real is real to us. This is where the real power of branding lies and is often overlooked. If branding can shape our perceptions, then perceptions are our reality. We have the power to create and shape our own reality and the reality of those around us.

Why do companies like Apple, Nike, and Cola-Cola spend millions of dollars on branding every year? The answer is simple: They are using the power of branding as the architect of their consumer's reality. The brand lives in the minds of employees, customers, the media, and everyone that interacts with the brand.

Armed with this information, let's start by clearly defining your target audience and crafting a marketing message that speaks directly to your ideal customers. This will begin the process of establishing a strong brand loyalty.

Hello Old Friend

If your brand was to talk, what would it say? Something I was told about as far back as high school English class when writing papers was to "define my voice." Defining your brand's voice and message is critical to your engagement with the world on social media. Your voice and message distinguish you as an individual and from others by conveying your brand's purpose, promise, and personality.

Humanize your brand voice and messaging and make it identifiable to your audience. In every instance in which your brand's voice is heard clearly, whether via social media posts, on your website, or other ads or marketing material, your brand voice should be recognizable, almost like recognizing an old friend's voice.

Fundamental truths about the essence of one of your friends can be simplified as the same reason people buy brands. Chances are, your friend's value system is similar to your own, which builds emotional goodwill and connection. It is well known that nothing happens until someone feels something, which I will talk more about in the linking phase of MBL. However, it's important to map before the value system that guides behavior can be linked to your brand's voice, image, and messaging. They should be cohesive and well defined. Having a guided strategy to define your brand as a person or converting your personal brand to well broken-down segments could be helpful and tighten up your marketing objectives and give you a more accurate picture of what you should share.

Social media gives everyone a voice. Who are you, and what does your brand stand for? Going through the process of re-discovering these things makes every marketing touchpoint more engaging, while providing a guideline or template will clarify the direction of content of all your future initiatives. Remember, a brand that stands for nothing won't provide any value or impact to the world, much less have any long-term success in a crowded marketplace.

Focus on defining:

- Purpose
- Vision
- Mission
- Values
- Objectives

In 2017, Sprout Social determined that the behaviors consumers want from brands on social media are:

- Honesty - 86%
- Friendliness - 83%
- Helpfulness - 78%
- Sense of Humor / Being Funny - 72%
- They are trendy - 43%
- Politically Correct - 39%
- Snarky - 33%

To give you a common example, think of Nike's brand voice. It's a shoe, and maybe now a clothing line, but when you think of Nike, you think of inspiring, positive, and maybe competitive. Their tone of voice is motivational and encouraging, and of course, urgent. A friend you want to have around that will push you to take action to achieve some athletic goal you aspire to achieve.

In our coaching workshops on "How to Use Personal Branding to Grow and Build an Audience and a Company," we go through a list of different exercises to sift through and boil down all the ingredients to form your brand's essence as well as your target persona.

Here are eight tips to help you define and sustain your brand's voice:

- Spend time defining the words that describe your brand
- "Voice" is a feeling when reacting to the words used
- Examine how your brand impacts the world and the people around it
- Consider what makes you attractive to others
- Ask what is your strength vs. what is not
- Make sure the brand can grow and adapt like a person
- Create consistency in every bit of content and copy with brand guidelines
- Amplify your brand's presence by focusing on only a few social channels

As you're starting to see, simply "sharing" content online is not as simple as it's made out to be.

You need to know and be aware of who and what your brand is. Not to mention the two-way engagement and co-creation of your brand's image through every like, share, review, public or private comment, and how you respond. Every conversation with every person who interacts with you or with your company directly or indirectly has a lasting impact. It guides the direction of your brand in the global consciousness that is forever documented online. The coming together of the social and technological systems are not developing independently in a vacuum; the two evolve together in complex set feedback loops, wherein each drives the other and leaves a footprint of everywhere it goes.

Linking

Now, most will agree that there are three ways to achieve growth: to increase the share of the markets you are strong in; to develop new products for those markets; then to expand to new markets. If only there was agreement on how one accomplishes these things. Traditional methods are no longer effective.

The world has shifted. Complexity has increased. Now, markets are conversations. People and companies are now brands. Coronavirus and social distancing have accelerated the transition of business operating online. Everything is upside down!

Not really, but kind of. At the core, we are all still the same. Maybe the platform or method we interact on is different, but we still have the same needs, wants, and desires. As hard as we try, we often make the majority of our decisions emotionally. Understanding people's state of mind and their aspirations and goals inspires creativity and relevance. This concept has always been a tenet of great marketing, but now true connection comes from engagement. It's driven by purpose and intention. What if you could establish an ongoing connection and **link** your prospects with the content they want at the exact time to help them make their purchase decision?

Creating content that aligns with the identity-based interests, passions, and desires of your target audience and then to subliminally put your products, services, or brand in the background of your content links your products to those emotions.

Most people are still busy trying to find the right viral video, infographic, or animated gif to generate the attention they are looking for and then trying to, for lack of a better term, "bait-and-switch" that attention to promote their product or service, rather than making it the core focus of the story of the message. I will also be the first to admit I was guilty of this as well because, for a long time, it worked, and because it worked, everyone continued to do it. It still works, to a degree, today, but people's attention spans have gotten so short that you have to connect the two. This is where some great advertising gets it wrong. You remember the ad, but not the product or service that is being promoted. You have to have the link!

For years, social media businesses were built on this attention-generating tactic and were scaled to the sky until

Facebook did an algorithm change and effectively popped that bubble. Now, attention is spread out all over the place, and new platforms like Tik-Tok are popping up, addressing the need for ever-shortening attention spans.

This again underscores why people need, when they see your brand, to know who you are and what you are about instantly. Brands need to represent the sum total of all aspirations and experiences for people who are in the brand's presence. When consumers hear your voice, they need to know it's you. This can only be done through consistent consciousness and repetitive brand messaging.

> *"Everyone thinks of changing the world, but no one thinks of changing himself."*
>
> - Leo Tolstoy

We need to evolve into an era of meaningful engagement and experiences to engage customers throughout the entire buyer's journey and create more relevant experiences to rise above all the noise. When we are cultivating relationships and increasing awareness, it all starts at the beginning of the relationship.

Start with empathy. Give with love. Listen. Expanding consciousness comes from seeing the value in all sides of an experience. Through sharing ourselves, we connect with the energy of the world around us.

Did you know that Gary Vee and other successful influencers and entrepreneurs still try to respond to each commitment on social media personally? He still replies to as many comments and messages as he can. I have also followed this path with much success. As the co-host of "The Unknown Secrets of Internet Marketing," one of the leading SEO podcasts that has been running for ten years with over 55,000 downloads a month, we try to thank and respond to everyone personally as well as acknowledge many live on the show.

Social Media is about connecting. Share, comment, like. If you want to capture people's attention, make them feel good and convey your personality. Align the messaging on your blog, social media accounts, email lists, and any PR with original content that is consistent with your brand's voice again and again.

Also, on another point, so many people are passive on social media or hold back sharing joy. Does it really cost anything to "like" or "heart" something? If you like one thing, does it mean that you have less likes to give next time? Of course not. Whatever you choose to share will be increased to you in abundance.

Brand Linking has a lot to do with psychographic positioning. Psychographic focus is on consumers' activities, interests, and opinions, not just the general demographic data, such as age, gender, or race, but understanding the cognitive attributes, such as customer emotions, values, and attitudes, among other factors. It's about transforming the decision-making process by linking the emotions to the way a brand makes them feel.

At one time in our lives, we all had a vision for a greater quality of life that we desired. Yet, for many, those dreams have become shrouded in the frustrations and routines of daily life. Your goal is to connect into that feeling they are seeking and show them how your product or service delivers on the promise that that feeling would give them.

If you're a jewelry store, "share" the feeling of love. If you're a gym, "share" the feeling of how a healthy lifestyle makes you feel or maybe the feeling of progress. If you're a travel agent, "share" the feeling of adventure and pleasure that travel gives. If you're a staffing company, "share" the feeling of when more efficient hiring practices help you hire the right candidate, and your life is easier because of it. Coca-Cola and Budweiser are masterful at this, and you can be too.

Think for a second, "Why would someone feel compelled to share in this moment with you?" Ask "why?" Ask "what?" Ask "how?" Think how engagement could be more relevant, more useful, more engaging. Connecting with others is where transformation begins. When you share your story with others, you not only speak life into people, you creating dynamic movement and growth.

The goal is to connect with the right people in the right words with the right content as they make their way through whatever decision process you want them to go through. Be purposeful. Focus on reaching your ideal customer with the right stories, in the right place, at the right time, being relevant and being persuasive, and your voice will be heard, and you will attract them to you!

How to Build A Memorable Online Brand with Chris Burres

When it comes to entrepreneurship, the adage, 'health is wealth' rings true.

Without a healthy body, your mind cannot perform at the optimal level necessary to run a successful business. And like the business world, you get what you put in. If you nourish and take care of your body, you will reap the benefits.

If you cannot work because of poor health, you can never be successful, and you are prone to making wrong decisions that can damage your business. If you're sluggish, distracted, or can't think clearly because of a cold or feeling run down, then it is hard to stay focused and deliver value to customers, the real key to success. Let's face it, a cup of coffee can give you a boost of energy, but it's not enough to make sure that you are healthy and can run a successful business.

Another crucial aspect of running a successful business is the ability to adapt to changing times strategically. Today - we all know that we now live in the digital or "information age." This historic time began in the 1970s with the introduction of the personal computer and subsequent rapid influx of technology. Now that it's the 21st century, everyone is online.

Fun fact: the rate of change will never be slower than it is today.

With the internet, access to copious amounts of information is easy and accessible to almost anyone. What does this mean? People are consuming, creating, and sharing information through the internet regularly. Therefore brands must create a powerful and compelling voice online. For the older generation, this shift in technology comes with a steep learning curve. For most, developing an effective digital brand marketing strategy is more manageable with expert guidance and patience.

My Story

For the past 25 years, I have been manufacturing carbon nanomaterials and selling them to research institutions around the world. My company pivot occurred in 2012 when it was realized that ESS60 is a nano-antioxidant that can stabilize free radicals. At first, we sold this product for research purposes only. Our customers were cutting edge biohackers, and they kept coming back to us with amazing testimonials about the benefits of ESS60. Our product is known to support the immune system in 5 powerful ways; it:

1. Is a known antioxidant, 172X more powerful than Vitamin C
2. Fits and conforms with anti-inflammatory diets, which have been associated with improved health and longevity
3. Is antibacterial
4. Is a known antiviral
5. Supports sleep, which improves your physical, mental, and emotional well being

Additionally, our most consistent testimonial is our customers take the product in the morning, they report mental focus and energy during the day and then better sleep that night. These testimonials and many more, are so powerful and so consistent that I decided to create a retail product based on the nano-antioxidant formulation. The product, MyVitalC, was launched 10 months ago and is on track to be a 7-figure business within the year.

Disclaimer: Though MyVitalC has not been tested on humans, ESS60 was found to increase the lifespan of rats by 90% - almost double their lifespan in a study published by Baati et. al. in 2012 at the University of Paris. This study used the MyVitalC formulation manufactured by my company. In addition to doubling the life span of the test subjects, when those test subjects died, they all died without tumors (unlike the control group who all died with tumors).

Here are a few marketing strategies and tactics that helped me grow my business that may be able to help you as well.

Develop A Unique Selling Proposition for your Business

For your business to stand out from the competition, you need to compete in the competitive nature of a unique selling proposition (USP). This will position your brand as an authoritative figure worth trusting. With the excess of information available at the tip of our fingers, it seems like every other business is doing great online.

In these moments, it's vital to remain confident. Choose to view the outward success of other businesses as nothing more than motivation to work on your online presence.

What is a Unique Selling Proposition (USP)?

In the book, *Build Your Brand Mania*, Matt Bertram defines a USP as:

"A basic guiding principle that helps you position your products or services in the marketplace. It is a finely-tuned offering to your clients or customers that no one else in the market can claim" (67).

How Can A USP Help Your Business?

In short, your USP is the message you share with the world to differentiate your brand from the rest. After all, if you fail to stand out from the crowd, how do you expect to attract the attention of prospective buyers? This is where your strategy comes in: You want your online presence to be unique enough to remember, but compelling enough to push people to take action (buy your products/service).

Your Value Determines Your Price

It's essential to do everything in your power to differentiate your business from the competition. The best way to be like everyone else is to think like everyone else. To counter this, you need to be methodical and strategic when branding your business online.

Remember: Never compete on price as there will always be someone willing to go out of business faster than you. Compete based on the value the product provides to consumers.

Be the "Bose Stereo" in the Industry

An example of a compelling USP put into action is Bose Stereos. If you're familiar with Bose Stereos, you'll know that they never go on sale. Yet, Bose is marketed and sold as one of the top products in the market. Throughout the years, the Bose music system has remained a very desirable product among consumers.

Let's take my company as another example. In our case, we're a research institution that has been around since 1991. We've been selling to other research institutions, which is a highly challenging and competitive market. What does this mean? It means that we have research technology and know-how to prove that our product is of the highest quality. We use this fact to increase the desire for our product over others, and we can charge a premium for the value we are delivering.

In other words, your USP message is successful when it positions your product/service as valuable, different, and of higher quality than the rest.

Establish Consistent Brand Messaging

Strong, clear, and consistent messaging is a great way to capture your audience's attention. At MyVitalC, behind all our messaging is a strong marketing strategy. Something I consistently say in almost every podcast and piece of literature or content online is:

> "We've been selling to research institutions around the world since 1991."

It is also important to develop a few key phrases for customers to remember your business. One of ours is "Feel healthy, live longer." Another is "Live Beyond the Norms." So, if you're a business building an online brand, set aside some time and jot down unique phrases, sentences, or words that accurately describe your brand. Most importantly, make sure the message you choose positively reflects your brand.

We have identified ourselves as the most trusted brand in our space. We reviewed our competitive landscape and we found fraud throughout our industry. This seems to parallel the supplement industry at large. One of the things we've done is to create videos that expose those fraudulent products in our industry to distinguish our brand from businesses looking to scam customers. This helps brand us as a trusted source for our product.

Do this exercise: Grab a piece of paper and write down everything your customers think of when they think of your brand. Make sure to keep their wants, needs, and desires in mind during the exercise. So many business owners get lost in their details and actually neglect the actual wants, needs, and desires of their customers. It is only from their perspective that you will be able to craft a compelling message.

Demonstrate High Levels of Integrity

In his book titled *The Millionaire Next Door,* Dr. Stanley interviewed millionaires and asked which factors contributed most to their financial success. The results found that *integrity* was the #1 top contributing factor. Here are the top five most contributing factors:

1. Integrity

2. Discipline

3. Social Skills

4. A Supportive Spouse

5. Hard Work

While all factors are essential to business success, there's a reason why integrity is at the top. The fact is, people want to buy from someone moral, ethical, and above all - honest.

The Greek Philosopher Aristotle narrowed persuasion into three fundamental appeals: ethos, pathos, and logos. He believed that ethics or ethos was the ability to convince an audience of the speaker's credibility or character. We all prefer to purchase from someone who is being honest with us. If you are going to be successful, you must address all three appeals. Combine these principals with the results of Dr. Stanley's surveys, and it becomes clear of the importance of having a brand that exudes ethos/integrity.

Determine your level of brand integrity by asking yourself these three questions:

1. Am I comfortable selling this for people to consume/use/wear, etc.?
2. Am I morally or legally able to sell it?
3. Does the price match the value of this product/service?

The answer to all three of these questions must be yes, no exceptions.

Define and Use Your Brand Voice

Brand voice is the way you talk to customers and describes your communication style. If you're trying to grow your online brand, spend some time identifying your Brand Voice. Ask yourself: What is the voice of my brand, and how are we going to share that digitally?

For my brand at MyVitalC, I started to engage actively and participate in conversations that were happening in the industry. We got involved in Facebook groups, and YouTube comments to showcase our voice and learn more about our customers. Make a plan, and create industry-related YouTube videos, share relatable memes, post current trends, and more.

All these actions help increase brand awareness and show a level of commitment and loyalty to your customers.

Call to Action

When you want people to act, you need to provide limited focus points. Research reveals that the more options, the fewer people buy, and their level of satisfaction is actually reduced.

In 2000, psychologists Sheena Iyengar and Mark Lepper published an extraordinary study that demonstrates this principle.

The researchers chose an upscale food market and set up a display table with 24 varieties of gourmet jams. Each person that sampled any of the jams was given a coupon for $1 off any jam. The researchers noted the total sales.

Next, on a different day, they set up a smaller table and display and distributed the same $1 discount to samplers. The difference this time was that there were not 24 varieties of jams but rather only 6 jams on the small table.

Which display do you think got more attention, and which one made the most amount of sales?

More people flocked to the large display and sampled the jams, but they were ten times less likely to buy than the people at the small table.

Too many choices and choices that are difficult or confusing paralyze the customer: He/she gets confused, does not know which one to buy, and ends up not buying anything.

The same is true for marketing calls to action - the final parts of marketing content that asks the user to take action: The more things you ask them to do, the more likely the prospect is to say no or click off the page.

Make the choice simple and make it easy to complete the action step.

Do you ever wonder why we say phone number's three-groups at a time? Or why you never remember the material you studied for when you cram it all into one night of studying? It is because when it comes to human memory - the simpler, the better.

So, determine a few main actions you consistently want to share with the world online that drive your customer to take action.

In the case of MyVitalC, we want people to purchase a subscription. All our marketing efforts are focused on driving people to subscriptions. When I am wrapping up an interview, I always share, "You can save 25% by going on subscription, and of course, you can cancel at any time." This consistent branded call to action has subscriptions responsible for 40% of our month over month revenue.

What do you want your consistent call to action to be?

Conduct Competitive Research

Spending a couple of hours a week researching what you're competitors are up to is necessary to stay up-to-date with the recent industry trends and news. Like it or hate it: Knowledge is power. Competitive research is useful because it shows you were on the rankings your company stands from an internet marketing perspective. For my business, I spend at least 5% of my time researching my competitors.

As much as you might hate to admit it, your company strategy isn't perfect. In fact, there are always ways to improve it. By evaluating the decisions and results of your competitors, you will learn how to plan for the future strategically. When you are doing this research, make sure you spend some of your time researching how products are different from the market you sell into. You might just come up with the next big marketing idea that revolutionizes your business.

Partner With an Internet Marketing Company & Value Continual Learning

If you're a business owner who understands the importance of internet marketing but is hesitant to work with an internet marketing company - you're not alone. Maybe you know people who have been burned by an internet marketing company, or perhaps you've been burned yourself. Maybe you want to make sure that you're branding your business online the right way, and yes, there are ways to do that.

First, try researching local reputable internet marketing companies. If you're looking for the best internet marketing company in the Houston area, EWR Digital, formerly known as eWebResults Marketing Agency, will do a phenomenal job. They helped MyVitalC grow rapidly, rank higher on Google, and positioned us as a first-mover in our industry! MyVitalC, with the help of EWR Digital, is already on track for 500% growth in 2020 over 2019.

Consider listening to podcasts, reading books, and watching YouTube videos about internet marketing. The EWR Digital podcast "SEO Podcast Unknown Secrets of Internet Marketing" is a great way to stay on top of internet marketing trends.

Hopefully, with these tips and a solid action plan, you feel empowered to scale a successful business, so it is time for you to take the reins and get out there! While it may feel like a daunting task at face value, once you break it down into small, achievable steps, your clients will recognize the quality and value your company provides, and they will demonstrate that recognition with the almighty dollar. Remember: Live Beyond the Norms

Take MyVitalC, for example. Our product is high quality, pure, and has created quite the buzz around Houston and beyond. Though it took time for our clients to see the life-changing effects our product offered them, eventually they couldn't live without it. In closing, if I provide one main takeaway for my fellow entrepreneurs, it's about building trust with your clients consistently and giving them what they need to improve their life. In other words, find your customer's pain points and do your absolute best to solve them to bring a smile to their face.

The Secrets of Selling with Billy Bray

Once you master the art of selling, business success is inevitable. However, many entrepreneurs fail to maximize the power of strategic selling. Why might you ask? The answer is simple: Not out of laziness, but out of fear. Fear of failure or rejection has deep psychological roots, and lack of confidence is the #1 way to lose a potential client.

> "Ninety percent of selling is conviction, and 10 percent is persuasion."
>
> -Shiv Khera

Luckily, I overcame my fear of public speaking and fell in love with sales from a young age.

Start Small. Dream Big. Take Risks.

When people ask how I found my passion for sales, I always attribute my parents.

They taught me to face my fears head-on, to never run from uncomfortable situations. I learned that the best way to conquer fear is through repeated exposure. Now, I embrace fear and make friends with it. I've found that tremendous confidence, strength, and courage come from doing what scares you the most.

My sales journey began at six years old. To help us face our fears of public speaking, my mother instructed my brother and me to go door-to-door selling ground cover plants to the neighbors for $2 a piece. We operated with the utmost professionalism, like two full-blown salesmen stuck in children's bodies. We even offered customers a money-back guarantee. If the plant died, we'd replace their item for free.

Every day, we filled up our little red wagon to scour the neighborhood for potential buyers. With lots of determination and hard work, our success grew.

Interpretation

All of us are afraid of something. Whether it's public speaking, heights, drowning, dying, or claustrophobia—fear is a normal human emotion. In many situations, fear is a good thing. Without it, we wouldn't survive for long. We'd run into traffic, leave our hands on hot stoves, and carelessly pet lions in the wild. In other words: fear is a great motivator, but only in certain situations. Fear only becomes a problem when we allow it to dominate our lives and control our actions.

> *"Fear is going to be a player in your life, but you get to decide how much.*

                                                          -Jim Carrey

By confronting my fear of public speaking, I discovered a strength of mine I wouldn't have otherwise. Where would I be today if I let fear dictate my life?

Door-to-door sales taught me how to:

1. Feel confident talking to people.

2. Transact business with others, even on a small scale.

3. Develop an entrepreneurial mindset from a young age.

Through prioritizing courage over fear, I developed the confidence necessary to pursue direct sales positions in the future.

The Keys to Business Success: Serve Others, Create Value, and Deliver Results that Improve the Quality of Life of Others

> *"Successful people are always asking for opportunities to help others. Unsuccessful people are always asking, "What's in it for me?"*
>
>   – Brian Tracy

Here's a mantra to live by: The more I can serve people, the more I will, in turn, be served.

As an entrepreneur, we're tasked to solve problems. So, start observing the world around you and taking inventory: Do you notice a problem that many people and or companies continually encounter? If so, great! The first step is complete. Now, start digging deeper…

If you're thinking of starting your own company, consider the following questions:

1. Is there a significant problem that my talent or expertise can solve?
2. Is there a demand for the product/service I am going to sell?
3. Do I personally believe in solving this problem?
4. Will solving this problem improve your customer's quality of life? If so, how?
5. How will I sell this product/service in an impactful way?

These questions help establish a customer-centric foundation for your company that is built to last.

The Rotary 4-Way Test

When faced with a difficult moral or ethical decision, I turn to this test for answers. The Four-Way Test was created in 1932 by Herbert Taylor, a member of the Rotary Club of Chicago. He was asked to take over Club Aluminum Company, which was facing near bankruptcy.

Taylor concluded that if he could convince his employees to do the right thing in every situation, their sales would increase—and ultimately save the plummeting business. One night, he drafted a 24-word code of ethics for employees to follow. The company survived thanks to this 4-Way Test philosophy.

It asks the following four questions: "Of the things we think, say, or do:

1. Is it the TRUTH?
2. Is it FAIR to all concerned?
3. Will it build GOODWILL and BETTER FRIENDSHIPS?
4. Will it be BENEFICIAL to all concerned?

How I Discovered My Brand

My passion for sales led me into other direct sales positions, including the insurance industry. I got a job working for a big multinational bank in their insurance unit. And my job was to work with bankers, analyze the company cash flow, and determine whether we could deploy our services and help clients.

While working in this position, I identified a major problem in the industry: Most people hate their insurance provider. People view insurance as a grievance because it's expensive, confusing, and often required by the law or bank. At this moment, a light bulb turned on in my head, and the solution was clear as day.

Create a Valuable & Rare Sale Situation the Customers Can't Resist

Shortly after this realization, I started my own company in the commercial insurance industry. I chose insurance because there's a massive market of people seeking help. When there's a vast market, there's typically a high demand. And, as market demand increases, so do the prices. Today—I've helped tens of thousands of people; that makes me happy.

In short: Supply and demand is a powerful business tool.

To meet this growing need, I partnered with a risk assessment Insurance Attorney and Health Insurance Broker. We offer a free initial consultation where we evaluate a company's policies, do a Due Diligence report, and decide if we can help them. We are always upfront. If we can't help, you will know. If we can, we explain to them how, then deploy the resources for optimal results.

We come together as a team and take a holistic approach. Together, we help our clients understand where their company insurance program stands. Almost **nine times out of ten**, we find problems, errors, duplications, gaps, high deductibles, and more. After the initial consultation, we come in and optimize these insurance programs—saving clients time and money.

Position Yourself as a Credible & "Trusted Advisor"

In the highly acclaimed *New York Times* bestseller, *Influence: The Psychology of Persuasion,* Dr. Robert B. Cialdini states:

"People find objects and opportunities more attractive to the degree that they are scarce, rare, or dwindling in availability."

Simply put: When you place an Insurance Broker (me) and an Insurance Attorney (my business partner) together—we offer a unique sale situation that's hard to refuse. We don't take Geico's, "We save you 15% in 15 minutes," approach. Instead, we take an intellectual approach, more from a consultative perspective.

People are more likely to do business with credible industry professionals with years of experience under their belt than a recent college graduate making empty promises. Let's be honest: Who would you trust?

In the book, *Build Your Brand Mania*, trainer, author, local keynote speaker and consultant in Digital Marketing and Social Selling, Matt Bertram, states, "People are often more willing to comply with a request or a recommendation when it comes from someone they perceive to be a legitimate 'Expert' or 'Authority' (9)."

Matt defines an "Expert" as someone who knows a lot about a particular subject, and an "Authority" as someone who is not only knowledgeable but also highly influential.

Using Online Marketing to Grow Your Brand & Boost Sales

The great sales trainer, speaker, and entrepreneur, Grant Cardone, once said, "The more reach you have, the more power you have."

If you only transact business with people you meet face-to-face, it's a difficult way to build a successful business. And it's an even harder way to scale a successful business fast. This is why establishing an online platform is crucial. An online platform acts as a conduit between you and your audience. It provides a quick and efficient way to access people in different cities, states, and countries.

We all have to realize that every five-year-old kid in America grows up with an iPad glued to their hands—and they know how to use it.

And, if I even want to stand a chance against these super millennials coming out of college, I need to work twice as hard to stay up-to-date with the latest trends on the market. If I don't get a head start on my competition, I won't stand a chance.

Don't Let Other People's Opinions Determine Your Future.

My last piece of advice is to remain true to yourself. Never let someone tell you that you can't achieve your dreams. A quote from Will Smith in *The Pursuit of Happyness* puts it perfectly:

"Don't ever let someone tell you that you can't do something. You got a dream; you have to protect it. When people can't do something themselves, they are going to try to tell you that you can't do it. You want something, go get it. Period."

The "Crabs in a Bucket" Mentality

Have you ever been in a situation where you told someone good news, and they responded in with a snide comment or shoulder shrug that made you feel undeserving of your recognition? Don't worry; you're not alone.

This is an example of the "crabs in a bucket" mentality. When you put multiple crabs into one bucket, an interesting phenomenon occurs. If one tries to claw its way out for freedom, the rest try to pull it back into the bucket.

Sad as it is, this type of mentality is common, especially in the work environment. While humans don't try to claw each other, they may try to dim the spirits of those as perceived as "above" them. Insecurity and jealousy are almost always at the core of such ugly human behavior.

Nothing Is More Important Than Self-Respect

At my last job, I was told that I didn't need to be a "celebrity" on the internet. My higher-ups refused to support me in my online marketing efforts financially. They forced me to take down my website, to stop promoting online content, and to stop recording my podcast.

How did I respond?

The next day, I quit my job.

Who was I to follow the orders of some washed-up, wannabe salesperson telling me my presence on the internet was foolish? And who knows where I would be today if I dared to listen to their advice.

Today, as an entrepreneur, I have the freedom to do whatever I see fit on a social platform to help grow my business. With hard work and determination, I have landed clients from Omaha, Nebraska, Newark, New Jersey, and Orlando, Florida. And I consult with them all through the internet from my home here in Houston, Texas.

Your Network Determines Your Net Worth with Nolen Davis

Many people know what networking is—others know what live streaming is—but few knew the power of both when used together!

Networking creates a large group of people to affiliate yourself and your business with for mutual benefit. Before social media, creating an interconnected and deep network was more of a challenge. Now, networking online can create leveraged exposure and build a brand at the same time. If you live stream a discussion with three business professionals in the room, it triples your ability to get *your* business noticed by *their* viewers. It also stays recorded for others to view later-- increasing your referrals, referrals, referrals exponentially in the meantime.

When you network with other business professionals on social media, it unleashes your full business potential; and everyone knows that there is strength in numbers. Creating video content organically increases engagement with the people in the room. Each person passes the live stream around, therefore creating a digital network online. Even better, if you share that video across multiple social platforms such as Facebook, LinkedIn, and Twitter, your brand awareness skyrockets!

This can be explained by a simple but powerful psychological tactic used in influence marketing. **The Mere-Exposure Effect**, also called the Familiarity Principle, states that "people tend to develop a preference for things merely because they are familiar. Meaning the more we are exposed to something, the more we will like it."

Hello World

Every entrepreneur has an origin story; mine began with a little book of inventions. As a young boy, every time a new idea popped into my head, I'd jot it down. Looking back, it wasn't so I wouldn't forget, but rather, so others would one day remember. I saw the world in a problem vs. solution mindset, always searching for creative ways to solve world problems.

When an idea surfaced, I would experience a rush of intense emotions. I felt a combination of excitement, euphoria, and fear — all motivating me to take action.

I soon realized, however, that nobody understood where my ideas were coming from. Even worse, nobody wanted to help me. In other words, encouragement was scarce and support was nonexistent. If you're in the same situation, here's a piece of advice:

"Stop Telling Your Big Dreams to Small Minded People."

-**Steve Harvey**

There are two ways you can respond when someone doesn't share or support your vision. Ultimately, there are two ways you can come out of any situation: either negative or positive. If you feel like nobody is there for you, you can either say, "This is a hard road to success, nobody helped me, let them get their own," or you can say, "Nobody is there for me, so I want to be there for everybody."

Trust me, I understand what it feels like to be alone, to lay awake all hours of the night with such a great idea, but no one to share it with. However, by going through this painful experience, I discovered my life purpose. If you want to learn how to share your brand story with the world through digital marketing and social networking, read on. I will teach you how to build a successful business from the ground-up.

This experience taught me many valuable lessons:

- **Perseverance amongst adversity**: Never give up in the face of a challenge. It's better to try and fail than to not try at all. Not trying at all typically creates regret.

- **Serve and promote fellow entrepreneurs**: Lift the spirits of other entrepreneurs by sharing my transformational story as well as listening to theirs.

- **Embrace failure with open arms**: Show me a successful entrepreneur who hasn't failed, and I'll show you a liar. Without failure, personal and professional growth is obsolete.

Through experience, trial and error, and falling forward, I learned a lot of valuable lessons along the way. Here are five that may help you scale your business:

1. Don't let the opinions of others distort your reality

As a child, my grandmother and I loved to cook spaghetti when I visited. We would boil the spaghetti noodles, drain the spaghetti in a colander for a few seconds, then put it back in the same pot. For me, this method wasn't efficient.

I began to wonder, "Why isn't there a pot with a lid that locks in place and allows you to drain the noodles without needing a colander? You could simply drain it right from the holes in the top, take the lid off, and voilà! Your spaghetti is ready. I shared this idea with my Aunt.

Her response: "There has to be *some reason* why they haven't made that yet. You just came up with the idea that it was *too easy*. There has to be something wrong with it, something flawed with it, or something mistaken about it.

She said to me, "That idea will *never* succeed. All the good ideas are already taken."

Flash forward a couple of years when my Aunt and I were sitting on the couch watching infomercials when the pot I described came on the TV.

I didn't subscribe to this limited way of thinking. Like all great leaders, I accepted the challenge and let it motivate me toward greatness. Now, once I have an idea, I commit to it 100% — all the way to completion.

Humans have an innate fear of failure. No one likes feeling uncomfortable or like being the outcast of the group. We are social creatures who thrive in a loving, supportive environment. So, when our close loved ones try to diminish our dreams, it isolates us and makes us feel foolish for believing in ourselves.

> The great Steve Jobs once said: *"Don't let the noise of other people's opinions drown out your inner voice."*

Successful entrepreneurs know this feeling all too well. However, they don't let it prevent them from taking risks. It's human nature for people not to understand someone who steps outside social norms to follow their own path.

People like structure and familiarity, both of which are in danger for the entrepreneurial visionaries. Learn to recognize when people scoff at your "unrealistic" ideas. Respectfully acknowledge their guidance and continue to focus on your purpose.

> *"The opposite of courage in our society is not cowardice...it's conformity."*
>
> **- Earl Nightingale**

Remember, as an entrepreneur, it's not your job to conform to others' opinions, but rather to inspire greatness in others. Deliberately seek out those who believe in your ideas and dreams. This will build your momentum and lead to greater future success.

2. The Power of Face-to-Face Live Interviews

One of the common questions my customers ask UpSocial Network is, "How do we magnify the brand voice and tell the story of the business at the same time?" We solve this problem by incorporating a face-to-face interview style in front of a live audience. This allows our clients to showcase their company's products or services and share their brand story in real-time.

"Why is this effective?" You may ask. The answer comes down to trust. When people organically hear your brand story in-person, it increases the chances they will relate to your brand.

Robert Cialdini, the author of *Pre-Suasion: A Way to Influence and Persuade*, states, "It's not just that people want to deal with someone they like. People also want to deal with someone who likes them and who is like them." Cialdini goes on to explain, "People trust that those like them who they feel won't steer them wrong."

So, when you share your brand story, products, or services live on-stage, you automatically solve the problem of capturing their attention. Further, the compliments, laughs, and applause do wonders for the social proof of your business.

3. Strategically Offer a Free Service

At UpSocialNetwork, we don't charge our clients to network with other entrepreneurs. We offer this as a free service because it allows us to protect our clients from being taken advantage of by greedy entrepreneurs who only want their products and move on to the next networking opportunity.

When people pay for networking, they feel entitled. You may think, "Oh, you owe me for this." My goal in providing this free service is to create a family-oriented environment full of people who truly want to build each other's businesses in person and digitally.

4. S.T.E.P. UP

I believe to successfully help each person in your networking group, you must find their superpower. Meaning, "What is their secret sauce?" Many people in the same industry try to accomplish the same thing, but what really makes them different is what makes their brand. If you know what their specialty or superpower is, it's much easier to refer business to them. Having one-to-one interviews allows me to ask questions that will really give me a chance to know my people.

I have an acronym that spells out your fingerprint on success. Each person's combination will be different, and it would be hard to find two people with the same combination. This acronym is

- S.T.E.P. UP
- Self Discipline
- Talent
- Experience and
- Purpose will

- Unleash your
- Potential

Because I do interviews with my team, I really listen for each of these elements, and again I doubt two people will be in the same industry. So let's break it down:

Self Discipline - Everyone knows that to get anywhere in life you have to have some level of discipline. So beating up on your craft is a given and is needed to evolve to the next level of any business, career, sport, etc.

Talent - Is your God-given talent, something that you can do better than most naturally without even trying. Most of the time, this talent is taken for granted because they have been able to do this their whole lives.

Experience or Environment - You grew up in a certain area, culture, and family. Everything you learned from all of those experiences taught you something different that you implemented in your life and use every day.

Purpose - Why are you here? What are you passionate about? What is your why? Your purpose is what you will storm the beaches for, sacrifice it all, and will be apart of your legacy.

That combination is how I learned to look at people, and because of that, I give great referrals to my members. This is what makes my networking group much more impactful than just giving business to each other. We create so many partnerships and alliances that grow our businesses along with long-lasting relationships.

5. Inspire & Lead a Successful Team

- **Love & Give Freely**: I believe that the best way to get is to give. If you don't have love for your team and try to further their business success, then you shouldn't be a leader. If you love your wife, you sacrifice. If you love your kids, you sacrifice. And, most importantly — as a leader, you *have* to sacrifice.

- **Treat Others with Respect**: Great leaders respect their team members. They understand that the best way to earn respect is to give respect. Otherwise, your team members will feel underappreciated and undervalued. Always aim to treat others as you wish to be treated.

- **Value Passion Over Money**: You can only live so long before the jig is up. With such limited time, I wouldn't start a business strictly for the money; instead, I would start a business from the standpoint of your passion. If your brand story is both passionate AND authentic, it will give you a huge leg up on the competition.

- **Stay True to Yourself**: Once you attain success as an entrepreneur, don't get so big that you forget where you came from. Sometimes, people get so caught up in their success that they forget all their failures and challenges along the way. They forget all the lessons they learned by *failing*, which ultimately their current success.

"Chase the vision, not the money, the money will end up following you."

- Tony Hsieh, CEO of Zappos

My Purpose

"I exist to serve by providing opportunities for people to reveal their greatness and inspire others through my example."

This is my purpose; to help others reveal their greatness. So everything I do from TV shows, radio shows, Guinness World Record Events, and networking events, are platforms that I create for my members to reveal their greatness. Networking is not just an action to build business. For me, it will be a part of my legacy.

How to Create a Digital Footprint in the Mortgage industry with Mortgage Mack

Purchasing a home is one of the most important decisions you will make in your lifetime. Put simply, quality houses are expensive; and many people need to take out loans to foot the bill. It is for this reason many seek out a trustworthy, reputable, and knowledgeable mortgage loan officer to help break down the complex home loan process so they can feel confident that they're receiving a loan best suited to their individual needs; this is where I come in.

As a mortgage professional for over 26 years, I've accumulated the knowledge and expertise to comfortably guide clients through the home loan process one step at a time. I have made a name for myself in the mortgage industry not out of luck; but out of years of experience, hard work, and consistently providing value to my clients.

My goal in writing this chapter is to share: how I made a break into the industry, advice for aspiring business savvy Mortgage Loan Officers, and how you, too can make a name for yourself in the digital age of social media. But, before we start, here's a little bit about me…

What I Do

I've been in the mortgage industry since 1996. My primary goal as a mortgage loan officer is to educate and prepare consumer for the process so it is as seamless and successful as possible. One of the main benefits you receive from working with a mortgage loan officer is the unique experience of one-on-one coaching myself and many other professionals make the most of in the industry. I work with the number one mortgage analysis software in the country with many of my buyers — especially buyers looking to refinance or move up to their dream home. The purpose of this is to ensure that I'm providing my clients with the correct information and guidance necessary to help reach their long- and short-term financial needs.

Over the past 26 years, I've helped so many people that I've had clients where I closed their first house 20 years ago and helped them buy their last house they currently reside in; I've even done loans for the grandchildren of many of my clients.

Overall, the main outcome I want for my clients is that they leave the mortgage loan process with these three outcomes:

1. A high level of understanding of the mortgage loan process

2. Reassurance that this is the right decision for them financially

3. Above all, my #1 most important job is to make sure that if the contract says we're closing November 10th, we close November 10th — end of story.

Tips for Homebuyers

#1. Be Organized

I cannot stress how important it is for homeowners to come prepared; the best way to do so is to start by putting all your financial documents together.

This may seem obvious, however — in my experience — organization is among the biggest challenge that most home buyers encounter. They don't know where their social security card is; can't find their W2 forms; they can't find their two-year bank statements or pay stubs; or have yet to file their tax returns. These are all problems that interfere and delay with a successful mortgage process.

Additionally, if you have any unresolved credit, bank statement, identification, or tax return issues you haven't dealt with in the past — it is vital to address those concerns before applying for a mortgage loan. At the very least, write a letter in reference to what those issues ever challenges were as a frame of reference.

#2. Ask The Right Questions

One of the most common mistakes I see homebuyers make not adequately preparing the right questions to ask their mortgage loan officers. Here's an example of a standard; yet broad question that lacks specificity: "What's the lowest interest rate?"

My problem with this question is that buyers unfamiliar with the mortgage industry often aren't aware that the lowest interest rate may not always be the lowest cost because of factors that come into play such as:

1. How long do you plan to live in the house in question.

2. Whether there are any discount points associated with the "low rate." The mortgage industry is no different than any other industry – the lower the price, the lower the quality of service.

#3. Check Online Reviews

If you Google "#mortgagemack", you will quickly find that I have over 30 five-star reviews, and can be found all over the first 3 page of Google. Why is this important? The answer is simple: If a lot of people love something — its probably for good reason. In other words: word of mouth, matters. Therefore, if you're looking to work with a mortgage loan officer and want to know if they are trustworthy, provide a reputable service that won't screw you over — I highly recommend sifting through their online reviews for reference.

Tips for Aspiring Entrepreneurs

#1. Be Solution-Oriented

What differentiates the average mortgage loan officer is my ability to solve problems. When I consult with each applicant, I try to spend at least an hour interviewing them on the phone and letting them interview me using the zoom video conference app. I've used video calls and conferencing for at least a decade. That way, when I visit with people and when I'm going through the numbers and process with them—they not only get to hear me explain the process, but they also get to see it live on their computer screen.

Even with the advanced technology of today, many mortgage loans officers still don't use the zoom video conference technology to engage with the consumer so they can discover and address their needs and wants, wants, desires. Actually, 93 percent of communication is "nonverbal" in nature. If you interact strictly over the phone, then challenges that are likely to occur during the process. I don't know about you, but from a buyer's standpoint, If I'm going to have a challenge—I'd like to know about it before we write a contract.

Home buyers often ask many questions to help ease the anxiety of such a large purchase. From my experience, the majority want to know two things:

    1. What's my payment?

2. How much do I need to close?

So, it is in the best interest of both parties for mortgage loan officers to know what they are talking about and remain attuned to the fears and questions of their clients every step of the process.

#2. Leverage Personal Relationships

In 2020, social media is an amazing tool for to foster strong relationships with clients and fellow colleagues. Today more than ever, you have to foster and bring immense value to the table and every relationship you encounter. It's not just about, "Hey, I've been doing this for 26 years," "Hey, I have this product, or, "Hey, we've close on time." In our fast-paced, technologically advanced generation— you really need to bring some added value to your relationships.

It's almost like we crave face to face interaction in today's traffic. I mean, its nearly impossible to have 2/3 appointments a day, and to get to all those appointments on time. People just don't have the time anymore to sit on the freeway going from one destination to another like we did a short 10-20 years ago. I think that may differentiate me—the way I try to step the process up with the consumer so there's a high level of understanding from the start. I would have a great deal of anxiety in the buyer's position and I'm in the business & know how it works!

#3. Utilize Podcasts in 2020 to Grow Your Brand Presence

Well, you know, the first search engine optimization podcast I ever listened to was The #1 Best SEO podcast on iTunes is SEO Podcast – Unknown Secrets of Internet Marketing by eWebResults.com by Chris Burres and Matt Bertram.

This podcast is full of useful strategies and knowledge. It covers everything from Internet Marketing, SEO, to AKA Search Engine Marketing.

Another primary influence that made me want to grow my online brand was the #AskGaryVee podcast from the New York Times best-selling author, motivational speaker, and CEO of multi-million-dollar marketing company VaynerMedia.

The first time I heard Gary Vaynerchuk I was inspired by his authenticity and true motivation for internet marketing. Gary was speaking at an event and he was talking about social media it's the new TV and how right now, it's expensive. He encouraged the crowd to take the first step and try to get as much attention using social media and the internet as you possibly can while it's still affordable.

His podcast made me believe that I could launch my brand on the internet from scratch.

Now, I've been on social media for a few years now creating and sharing new content. I'm on a radio show on a regular basis called the **Real Estate U Show**.

#4. Never Underestimate the Power of Word-of-Mouth & Referrals

To this day, I get the vast majority of my business from real estate referrals and my 6,000 past clients.

Having a presence on the internet is important — even if you don't get direct ROI on it, right. In other words, people don't go Google mortgage Mac if they want a home loan; but if they're referred to me — they're going to go look me up on the internet. You know they are; and if helps if you have a presence.

Having an online presence matters more than if you were to have the best website in the world. At the end of the day, if your clients aren't happy and your name is associated with thousands of negative reviews on Google, your trust and reputation will suffer greatly. As much as it sucks, people trust people more than they trust a manufactured website.

In my case, I have people come up to me all the time and say, "I looked you up on Google. I see that you have over 30 five-star reviews. For example, I know that if I Google the keyword "Loan Officer Houston" right now, that my face will be the first one on the maps — and that's a significant advantage to have over your competitors.

#5. Find a Mentor

Along with having online mentors you look up to in the digital space such as Matt Bertram, and Gary Vaynerchuck, it's also important to find a real world mentor to collaborate with. For me, that mentor was Mark Lacour. He works as the editor-in --chief editor of Oil and Gas Global Network. When we met, we were just workout buddies. However—as we grew closer—we started talking about business and he told me he planned to go in the digital direction. This sparked my interest, and I soon realized the power of social media in business thanks to him. He was the first person to get me motivated to engage with a digital footprint and use search engine optimization, Facebook, LinkedIn, etc. To this day, I admire his leadership and guidance in my own career. I strongly encourage you to listen to his extraordinarily successful video blog called Modal Point that has garnered tens of thousands of oil and gas listeners on a weekly basis.

I'm in sales, and he's in sales. And in sales—time is money. If you can reach out and contact somebody with a Podcast, Facebook live post, or YouTube video—you instantly have the ability to impact a dozen, hundred, or even a couple thousands of individuals! With face-to-face, on the other hand—you simply can't reach that many people at once.

Mark traveled all over the world for his job and realized how tiring it was to go to such great lengths just to meet face-to-face with one person. Now, he reaches thousands of tens of thousands of people with his podcast and it generates sales for him.

Build Your Online Presence with Social Media

I will conclude with this story: I got my first cell phone in 1992 when I was in my twenties. It was a big, old cell phone; far from a fashion statement. Back in the day, we used to carry pagers for work that made you call-in to check your messages from the receptionist. But if you look at then, to now — you see just how much times have changed; and how technology has driven that change.

Before the invention of the internet, my ability to market my brand to the masses was severely limited in comparison to the opportunities for growth made available today through the advancement of technology. I remember back before the internet, my brand was secluded to the relationship's I could develop through one-on-one emails, phone calls, or face-to-face conversations. Overall, branding your business was much more simple; but that came with a caveat. When systems are too simple, it limits growth.

Now, through using Facebook Live, Instagram, LinkedIn, Email Marketing, Podcasts, and so much more, the internet has given me the opportunity to broaden my sphere of influence all through the click of a button. While the complexity can at times be a bit overwhelming, the pro's far outweigh the cons. It has allowed me to connect with thousands of like-minded business professionals across all industries and continents. Considering the sheer opportunity of growth available through social media and the internet today — I wouldn't change it for a thing. In fact, I look forward to what technology has to bring in the future for business worldwide.

Build a Strong Foundation for Your Business with Randall Chesnutt

I am the owner of the direct response marketing agency, Spoken About. We were very strategic about why we chose the name Spoken About in particular, to represent our brand. At the end of the day, every entrepreneur wants their business to be "Spoken About." But, only very few capture the attention of the masses. So, what separates the tigers from the sheep? You might ask. Well, in this chapter, I plan on answering that question one step at a time. Before we start, if you're a business owner—whether that be for a startup, medium-sized company, or fortune 500 company—and looking for a full-proof method to generate a "buzz" about your business, it is crucial that you first learn how to strategically craft your message to your target audience in a way that resonates with those people. Trust me, it's easier than it sounds.

You tell one friend, they tell another, and it proliferates out. You know the saying, "The pen is mightier than the sword?" Well, in this instance—word of mouth is mightier than paid advertising. Remember that. We'll look deeper into that later in this chapter. But, before friends can share all the wonderful things you can do for them, you first you have to understand your business to the *core*. This includes knowing everything about the *Who, What, and Why* of your company.

- Who are you going to serve?
- What are you going to offer them?
- And, why should they choose you (or your product) over everything else on the market?

Once these basic questions are roughly answered to the best of your abilities — then, you can speak with a marketing agency company like Spoken About. At that point, your job is done, and now it's time for us to do our job. We only ask for this stipulation for a very basic reason: How can you expect us to help market your company if you don't fully understand what your company has to offer? Now — if you're new to the world of marketing agencies and how they can help your business — then as fasten your seatbelts; you're in for a bumpy ride.

The Purpose of Marketing Agencies

When you partner with a marketing agency like Spoken About, they help you craft a message and get that message out to the right audience to capture their attention through various mediums. Namely — through digital or print mediums. If you are curious about whether a marketing agency can help your business or not, here's an example of a someone who would benefit from using our service.

Let's suppose you wanted to build your own house. You wouldn't walk up to a builder and say, "I want a house." First—you would need a blueprint. That would be the same as if you didn't have a house, and you asked a contractor to build you a bathroom. This wouldn't work because he simply wouldn't have enough information to do his job. Before you can build a bathroom, you first need a house to build the bathroom in. Likewise, the same rules apply if you asked needed someone for Search Engine Optimization (SEO) but didn't have a website to run keywords and optimize rankings. Before we can use SEO keywords—we need to understand your business to know what it is you do so we can incorporate the right keywords to route traffic to your business.

That's where we come in; we specialize in helping customers build marketing blueprints based-on the trajectory of where their business will go to in the future. Once we have your company name, the problem you specialize in solving, and who your target market is—then we come up with the target message and ad campaign to generate new leads. So, it's not as easy as, "Let's go run a YouTube Ad; it's much more complex than that. Marketing agencies also control and manage:

- SEO (keywords driving people to the offer)

- Where do you want customers to go once they click on the Ad? Perhaps an offer? Then you need to determine what's the offer.

- Once customers click on the offer or information you're promoting on the Ad, then they need to have a "follow-up," Who's going to control the follow-up emails or calls?

- Who's going to control Google Analytics?

At the end of the day, even if we drive a million people to your page to show them the website content "proving" how awesome you are—that isn't enough to drive potential customers to pick up the phone. Especially if there's no call to action (CTA), people won't know what to do with the information given to them—and they'll probably click off your page in search of another marketing agency that's directly telling them what actions to take.

Ultimately, Spoken About is the architect of your company; meaning, we design the blueprint built on a solid foundation. And, based on your openness to hire the best marketing agency—depending on your budget—we work accordingly. For example, if you were looking to buy a house with a budget of 5,000,000,000, then there's a lot more we can do with your home than if your budget is only $5,000. Therefore, if you say you want to work a top-notch marketing agency like Spoken About, you can expect the price to match the quality.

For a new re-brand strategy requiring a new website, you can expect high-quality marketing agencies to charge anywhere between $5,000-$10,000. For top-notch SEO: $10,000 a month. And for building out quality video content: $5,000 per project. You also need to consider the following and work that into your budget:

- Who's going to run the Facebook? And how much do to intend to spend on that?

- How much for YouTube Ads?

The Benefits of Working with a Marketing Agency

When I sit down with each client, my main goal is to build a blueprint custom-made for their business and help them understand how it will work. I help clients of all sizes and prestige. I work anywhere from start-up companies to mature business owners already making money, but starting to have frustrations about running their business.

First, starting out, we take the time to sit down with you to discuss any needs, issues, and concerns about your business. In addition, we also allow you to interview us to ask us all the questions about our process and how it works. After this, we will fully-understand your company needs, and will create a blueprint accordingly. Many times, our customers begin to notice that departments have trouble working seamlessly together. Perhaps sales and marketing aren't working cohesively, and it's our job to bridge those gaps once we understand how each piece of your company works together. While it is an option to hire a different contractor for Marketing, Advertising, Sales, etc., we just don't advise clients to take that route because its difficult to determine who's good and who's not. In the end, our team wants to become the agency that handles each part of your business to make sure it's functioning at it's at an optimum level.

There is No "Magic Bullet" Solution in Marketing

The most common misconception for anyone in marketing or advertising is that people assume there's one "magic bullet." I hear people say things like, "I just need to run this one YouTube Ad" or "Facebook Advertising will solve all my problems." Sadly, however—that isn't the case. On the surface—yes—it is just a YouTube ad. But, there are all kinds of working parts behind it driving its success. Simply put, YouTube is one of *many* vehicles to get traffic. Others include:

- Email campaigns
- Automated Follow-Up Emails
- Facebook Ads / Marketing
- Video Marketing
- Lead Generating Websites
- Marketing Automation
- Pay Per Lead (PPC)
- Mobile Marketing
- Analytic Call Tracking

Sometimes the bad thing is when you're running a Facebook Ad is that it does work. The caveat—however—is that it typically only works for a short amount of time. Further, if you only run Facebook Ads, it's much easier for your company to turn into a commodity quickly. How, you might ask?

The answer is simple: When you only rely on Facebook ads—for example—your competitors can see what you're doing and easily copy it. And soon, everybody's doing what you're doing, and you've lost your originality and value on the market. On the flip side, only a small percentage of people are focusing on SEO, YouTube Ads, and Google AdWords because they're much harder to implement in terms of ROI successfully.

Create a Clear CTA (Call to Action)

When people Google your information online, you need to have a strategy in place. If you currently have a website page, you need to ask yourself: How am I encouraging viewers to give me their information? For example, if you go to an attorney's website, you're probably interested in understanding one of the following:

1. How much is child support going to be?
2. Legal advice if I'm in the middle of a divorce?
3. For females—when am I going to get paid?
4. For males—how much do I have to pay?

In this situation, the job of a marketing agency is to present the answers that the client is desperately searching for—front-and-center, in a clear view. Ideally, you want your answers to solve the viewers problems as quickly and effortlessly as possible.

To accomplish this, I would put a calculator for viewers to calculate an estimate of how much you'd have to pay. Or, address payment concerns for men by posting a blog titled, "The 5 Things All Men Should Understand About Divorce." For women, perhaps publish a blog titled, "Advice for Newly Divorced Women," you get the picture. As cold as it seems, people are too busy and lazy to read—let alone *care* about what school you went to—or how many awards you won in law school.

The only thing they want to know when they land on your page is: **Can they solve my problems**? It seems so obvious, but you would be surprised at how many business websites forget to think about the needs, fears, and desires of the clients before publishing content online.

Address Client Fears Using the "Aha Moment"

How do you help clients get past their fears? Many fellow entrepreneurs ask me. My answer is always the same:

I lead clients in the right direction until they eventually reach an "aha moment." What exactly is an "aha moment," you may ask? The "aha moment" is a moment when the client suddenly realizes how their company is missing the boat.

If you've watched TV in the past year—chances are—you might be familiar with the name Mike J. Lindell. Ringing any bells? Mike Lindell is commonly referred to as the MyPillow founder who went from a crack addict to a self-made multimillionaire. Today, he's sold a shocking 30 million pillows, and revenues have grown from around $100,000 a year to close to $300 million.

How do you think Mike Lindale sold millions of dollars in pillows when we can easily get at Walmart, Kohls, Macy's for half the price? The answer is easier than you think: It's because he came up with a blueprint for selling pillows and he asked you to buy a pillow. Simple as that. All he had to do was put his face on an ad—hugging the pillow and say, "These are the Best Pillows You'll Ever Own," in his infomercial. He then went on to explain all the problems most people have with their pillows. How most buy pillows that are too hard, or too soft—and positioned MyPillow to be "just right." He then sealed the deal by saying, "Call, or go to mypillow.com now, and Mike will give you two MyPillow premiums for one low price. I personally guarantee MyPillow will be the most comfortable pillow you'll ever own, or your money back." It's almost as if he took a page straight out of the "The Three Little Pigs" children's story to a tee.

The truth is—every business has that exact same opportunity. When you sit down with a client who's serious about wanting to grow their business, I almost always tell them a story like that. It's during those moments when they usually have their "aha moment" of clarity. Then, I typically explain how there is no "magic bullet" in marketing. Instead, I tell them that successfully marketing their business will be a lot of hard work; but that it's going to reward them thousand-fold. All they have to do is stick it out and invest a lot of time, patience, and money for the best results possible.

Creatively Solve Your Customer's Problems Using the PQAS Acronym

I started my career in the concrete business. Soon, however, I realized how tough the industry was, and decided to partner with a company outside of Tennessee to start doing decorative concrete. Starting out, I encountered a problem: I had the idea to *show* potential clients a cobblestone template on their driveway to prove how beautiful it would look. So, I decided to spray a really thin layer of concrete on the color to make it look like they had cobblestone on their driveway. Soon, however, I realized how difficult it was to see what their driveway would actually look like if they bought the service.

After some creative problem-solving, I took a risk and hired a photoshop guy. I then proceeded to go door-to-door through the entire neighborhood and took pictures of their houses. Next, I instructed the photoshop buy to put pictures of three different driveway designs (cobblestone, brick, and granite) onto each of the driveways of the houses. Then, I put a flier on the front door of every one of those houses with the CTA: "If you want your driveway to look like one of these three — call me." Long story short, I got so busy, and I sold the business. Here's a breakdown of my business acronym PQAS I created for situations like the following for you to apply it to your own scenario:

> **Problem**: I need to make money paving cobblestone driveways, but don't know how to stand out to my target audience and prove that my service is worth paying good money for.

Question: How can I convince my target audience (neighborhood house residents) to pay to have me pave a cobblestone driveway?

Answer: Create an image of three beautiful cobblestone driveway options using photoshop, post it on their door, and give a clear call to action telling them to call me if interested. Use the power of an image to show potential customers what it could look like if they work with you. In other words, do everything you can to create an offer they can't resist.

Solution: Ugly driveways☐ beautiful driveways. In conclusion: Happy customers and money in my pocket.

If you're someone to often struggles addressing, and or knowing how to the problems of your target audience — you're not alone. For this, I recommend using the PQAS system to break down the big picture into simpler, more manageable steps. At first, I didn't understand how easy the process was until I tried it, and it worked. All I had to do was:

1. Notice a neighborhood with a large proportion of unfavorable driveways
2. Show each customer what it *could* look like
3. Further convince them by marking the service at an affordable rate and promising only to take five hours to complete the project.

Once I did that, **almost every customer called me**; not all of them bought, but almost everybody said they loved the cobblestone. If only they had the money — they would buy it.

To those people, I would offer a financing plan for them to pay $100 a month, which was usually enough to seal the deal.

Once You Find a System that Works — Apply it to a New Business Idea

After the cobblestone business turned out to be a success, I took the same concept and built a credit repair business where I made $2,000,000,000 using the same blueprint applied to a different scenario. In this scenario, I went directly to the person who had to tell people no; we didn't actually go to the consumer at all. We made this decision because nobody cares about their credit until somebody tells them no. Most people don't walk around thinking, "I wonder what my credit score is?" The only time they wonder about that is if they're in the store shopping and the cashier says, "You can get 20% off your purchase if you get a credit card" — and you're told — "There's no way you can get approved with your credit score." Or, if you're making a big purchase like buying a house or a car.

Instead, we reported directly to the mortgage lenders at the banks and said, "Hey, you're going to have these people come in and try to make a big purchase. However, you're going to have to tell seven of the ten no because it revolves around their credit score." Then, instead of telling the customers with bad credit, "no," we told the lenders to say instead, "It's not a no; it's a not yet. Can I connect you with someone who I think could get you there?" Can you guess who those people were? Those with bad credit would report directly to my team where we would and help them work toward getting a good enough credit to buy a house, car, what have you.

Once again, we just kept using the same call to action—and attached it to something they want. In this instance, the only problem was that their credit sucked—and we specialized in fixing credit. Problem solved.

If you think about everything you've ever bought in your life, it comes down to the following: **What do they need, and how is this product a solution?**

How I Got into the Marketing Agency Business

And that's when I had my own "aha moment" that started my journey in the marketing agency business. I thought of the idea: Why don't we start buying businesses with poorly functioning business systems in place—ones needing a marketing company to drive the traffic. From there, we began buying gyms and quickly turning them into a profit and selling them.

We decided to start buying gyms because they were an extremely profitable choice in the market. For those who don't know, gym owners, many times, are responsible for almost everything. Because of this, gym owners easily get burned out from conducting the classes, cleaning the gym, closing up every day, doing the books, and calling on the receivables. After a while, they inevitably get tired of working overtime and wanted out. They would put the gyms on the market for cheap, and my team would save the day with one of our proven marketing systems. At that time, Facebook Ads were making a killing. So, we'd run a few ads, drive traffic, generate leads, and report back to the owner. We'd say, "If you want to—you can still run the classes or clean the gym.

But, we've built a system that only requires you to run a business that's in the fitness space you believe in—and everything's already done for you. 9/10, we were met with a resounding "Yes!" and a sigh of relief.

When You're Afraid to Take a Risk: Don't Think too Much; Just Do It!

In college, I studied Human Behavior. To my surprise, a lot of what I learned can be applied to my work today. When broken down, marketing is simply understanding how the mind works.

Throughout my college career, I learned a lot about the brain—particularly neuroscience and how that's tied to human motivation.

A common question people wonder when it comes to human motivation is: Why do we procrastinate? Especially when the most maddening part of it all is that we all know what we *should* be doing, so why aren't we doing it?

I learned that people don't procrastinate typing up a document in a literal sense. Instead, they procrastinate the *stress* that their mind doesn't want to experience involved with typing up a letter of resignation document, for example.

Let's take skydiving, for example. Anyone who's been skydiving knows that the instructors almost always jump on "two" instead of "one-two-three, JUMP!" The reason they jump early is to prevent people from thinking too much about it and starting to panic. The inability to think through actions that frighten us robs the mind from the chance to think too much about it—and forces it to face the fear.

When I was a kid, my friends and I used to jump off this bridge that was 60 ft. high. When you're in the water, 60 ft. doesn't look too high. But trust me—once you get up there—sheer panic starts to set in as you begin to think about everything that could go wrong in that moment. Because of this, if you ever got to the top and waited for longer than five seconds—you would never jump. Your mind simply wouldn't let you. So, every time I got up there, as soon as I looked over the ledge—I jump; that's the way I do everything in life. I analyze a situation, think about the risk level—then **just do it**.

Are things going to happen that I don't want to happen? Almost always, things rarely go exactly as planned. But the key is to trust yourself and your skill level enough that you can fix almost anything that happens. Why bother worrying about what is; or isn't going to happen—just do it and when those things go wrong—fix them. And try to avoid repeating past mistakes in the future.

Unfortunately, in life—some things are out of your control. But, you do have the ability to control is how you react when unfavorable circumstances are thrown your way. Are you too afraid to start a business out of fear of what people might think, whether it will fail, or whether you will make a fool of yourself? STOP overthinking it. If you really want to do it, just do it and pick up the pieces that are bound to crumble along the way. You will end up stronger and more courageous than most people ever dare to be in this world.

If You Mess Up, Are You Going to Fix It?

A lot of companies are nervous about getting negative testimonials. Well, I have some truth to say to everyone. First of all: If you don't have a lot of testimonials, most likely, you just don't have enough customers to find the crazy one. If you work hundreds or thousands of clients, there's no way that you're going to be perfect *every time*. It's just not possible. Of course, if there's many negative reviews, then that doesn't reflect well on the company. In my opinion, when someone goes to read reviews, and they encounter a negative one — what they really want to know is: If they mess up, are they going to fix it?

In other words, if there is a negative review and the company didn't answer — well, that answers the question. On the other hand, if the company answers and doesn't try to blame the customer, even if it was their fault and says something along the lines of, "Hey, give us a call, we want to make it right, maybe we dropped the ball, and we want to fix it." So, the customer reads their response and thinks, "Well, maybe they did or didn't mess up, but if they fix it — that's all I care about."

If You Aren't Confident in What You Have to Offer — Who Else Would Be?

My favorite testimonial that I've ever seen wasn't a testimonial for me, but a testimonial for a business we helped build for a client. The testimonial was a before and after for a fitness client in her mid-50. I wasn't deeply affected by this testimonial in particular because she had lost a lot of weight;

you could tell she lost a little but not much. Instead, it was the look on her face that made this testimonial burned into my memory for years to come. If you look from the before picture to the after picture — she had so much more confidence in the second picture than thefirst. And, it doesn't end there. I was reading through the comments and found this comment she wrote:

> "My husband took this picture. It was the first time in 25 years of marriage that he said I looked beautiful."

This comment made me take a step back for a moment. It was suddenly so apparent as to why her husband likely never told her she looked beautiful (even though every woman of all shapes and sizes deserves to be called beautiful). It was because **confidence exudes beauty; and that's what she had been missing all along**. In today's society, women are told you have to have a perfect model body — and that's just not true. What makes an individual attractive is that they're confident in who they are as a person. There's just something about that revelation that's just magic.

From my experience, I've found that usually when someone's insecure, they start relying on others to make them happy. If only they would realize that happiness can only come from within, and they have the power to unleash that happiness.

The same concept applies to business. When a business is confident in what they're doing and has a plan for the future — it is then that they'll have their "aha moment." Usually, when a client comes to see me, and I can tell that they're not confident in what's going on in their business, I automatically know that their clients aren't either. The reason being: If the business owner has no confidence in the business, then they'll most likely have no idea what criteria they are being judged on. This leads to employees feeling as if they could be fired at a moment's notice. In short, insecurity is contagious.

True Confidence is a Skill That Only the Patient and Determined Inherit

You may be thinking to yourself, "Okay, that makes sense. How can I develop the confidence I need to make my business successful?"

The tricky thing about confidence is that it is a skill that requires an immense amount of practice and patience. You can read all the books in the world about box somebody, but you don't *really* know how confident you're going to be until you're placed into the situation. For example, until you get in the ring with a fist headed straight toward your face and a hulk-sized man running straight in your direction will your knowledge and skills be put to the test.

In the digital marketing book, *Build Your Brand Mania*, author Matt Bertram encourages entrepreneurs to just "Go for it," and uses the example of one of his favorite online gurus, Seth Godin. He states, "Essentially, Godin states that you can't get good at anything by toiling away at it in your safe little basement hideaway. He goes on to explains that to get noticed, you need to emerge from your "Fortress of Solitude" and to "Show the world what you've got; this is about getting out of your comfort zone. There's no perfect time; there is only now, and now is precisely the time when you need to start putting your brand into effect" (70). Essentially, Matt is explaining why it's important to take action if you want to gain confidence and achieve your business goals.

Knowledge and Capacity Are Useless in the Absence of Real-World Experience

There's an iconic scene in the 1997 film *Good Will Hunting* that explains the difference between "toiling away in your safe little basement hideaway" and taking action in the real world, which is crucial for an entrepreneur's success.

The film's main character Will Hunting—currently a janitor at MIT, has an undiscovered inherent genius IQ. One day, Will sneaks into a classroom to solve a graduate-level math problem, and his talent is noticed by Professor Gerald Lambeau, who decides to mentor Will to help him reach his full potential. Later in the film, Will is arrested for attacking a police officer; and Professor Lambeau pleads his deal if he compromises and meets with a therapist for treatment. Unwillingly—Will agrees; but tortures every therapist he encounters with his sarcastic, smart-alec comments and skillfully dodges any real conversation by deflecting questions back onto the therapist as a defense mechanism. He runs through multiple therapists until one—Sean Maguire (Robin Williams)—see's through his act. On one session, Will is trying to get a rise out of Sean by probing about his ex-wife and why they got divorced to avoid delving into his troubled past. Sean reacts and calls out his real-world ignorance and says the following:

"If I ask you about women, you'd probably give me a syllabus about your personal favorites. You may have even been laid a few times. But you can't tell me what if feels like to wake up next to a woman and feel truly happy. You're a tough kid...I'd ask you about love ...you'd probably quote me a sonnet. But you've never looked at a woman and been totally vulnerable, known someone that could level you with her eyes, feeling like God put an angel on earth just for you, who could rescue from the depths of hell. And you wouldn't know what it's like to be her angel, to have that love for her, be there *forever*, through anything. You don't know about real loss, 'cause it only occurs when you've loved something more than you love yourself. And I doubt you've ever dared to love anybody that much." -Robin Williams, Good Will Hunting

In the scene above, Sean can tell Will is only paying lip service to act like he knows everything about the world when he doesn't. In business terms, Will would be the same as a haughty 18-year-old entrepreneur creating a perfectly curated website raving about everything his company can do, yet has no real experience, testimonials, or references to show for it. As the overly-used, but the true saying goes: Talk is cheap. Or—as many best friends advising their girlfriend dating a loser who always says he loves her but never takes her out on dates—actions speak louder than words.

Before you judge a business from their empty promises online, you must first ask: What is the foundation of this business? Just like Will's weak foundation—if the foundation is hidden under a "fake" exterior—it is only a matter of time before it cracks and crumbles. All it takes is the right person or life to take its course to finally expose the business for what they truly offer to customers. Nevertheless, what we know for sure is that the foundation for every business is its owner. However, the only thing that separates the weak versus the strong business owners is whether or not they willing to do what it takes to make the business successful. If business owners aren't willing to put in the work, then I usually don't take those people on as a client.

Beware of Bosses Who Don't Value Their Employees

One thing I don't appreciate is working with bosses who don't value their employees as much as I believe they should. These bosses are easy to spot from a mile away. In fact, I can tell by how they respond in this scenario: I'll usually walk them through a system and say, "Okay, here's the front desk person. She's one of the most important aspects of the company." The bosses who don't value their employees will quickly cut me off and say, "Ehhh, I don't know about that."

To me, this shows a lack of thought and overall apathy for their company as a whole. This type of response tells me that they don't understand what we do at Spoken About. Why? Because if you generated a call and the front desk girl goes, "Hello!" in an abrupt manner, it immediately sets the tone off on the wrong foot. But, if she answers in a calm, upbeat manner and says, "Good morning, it's another great day at XYZ company, how may I direct your call," your client on the phone will be more likely to respond to what you have to say positively. Then, if you train them to say, "Are you a current client, or are you looking for information?" you can transfer the call to the corresponding employee trained to help their particular problem their calling about. And you already know that if an employer doesn't value the little stuff, it's a clear indication that the big stuff won't work.

Provide an Easy-to-Understand Solution to Your Customer's Problems

For example, when Steve Jobs came back to Apple the second time, they were 90 days away from going out of business, meaning—we would not have iPhones right now. Jobs came in and told Apple to scrap everything they were doing and focus on something called an iPod. All of the employees responded with, "What's that?" even though the product was already out there.

In fact, many companies – including Diamond, Creative Labs, and Sony – sold their own MP3 three players years before the iPod hit the market on October 23, 2001. The major caveat, however, was that no MP3 players before the iPod could play major hits. In 1999, Creative Labs Nomad had 32 MB of memory (enough for about 1 or 2 CDs at low quality) for a whopping $429. Other than that, music on the digital market was minuscule. For reference, here's a snippet shared on their history page about the announcement:

JANUARY 2000

Announced two new additions to its Personal Digital Entertainment (PDE) solutions - the **NOMAD® Jukebox** and **NOMAD® II MG**. Both products include USB support, are programmable and support multi compressed audio formats including MP3 and WMA. With a 6GB storage capacity, Nomad Jukebox can store over 100 hours of digital audio.

So, why was Apple's release of the iPod what finally "broke" the world of digital streaming? For comparison, here's a clip of Apple's release of the iPod:

Apple Presents iPod

Ultra-Portable MP3 Music Player Puts 1,000 Songs in Your Pocket

CUPERTINO, California—October 23, 2001—Apple® today introduced iPod™, a breakthrough MP3 music player that packs up to 1,000 CD-quality songs into an ultra-portable, 6.5 ounce design that fits in your pocket. iPod combines a major advance in portable music device design with Apple's legendary ease of use and Auto-Sync, which automatically downloads all your iTunes™ songs and playlists into your iPod, and keeps them up to date whenever you plug your iPod into your Mac®.

"With iPod, Apple has invented a whole new category of digital music player that lets you put your entire music collection in your pocket and listen to it wherever you go," said Steve Jobs, Apple's CEO. "With iPod, listening to music will never be the same again."

Looking at the two announcements side by side — it's clear why people chose Apple over Creative Labs. The primary reason being: Creative Lab's required people use programmable support to "compress audio formats including MP3 and WMA. And at the time, nobody knew what an MP3 was — let alone how to compress it using a program. It would be like if someone today asked you to get this flux capacitor.

You'd most likely respond with, "What the hell is a flux capacitor?"

Jobs, on the other hand, said that the people that we're looking for are the people that have those CD's under their seats, CD's on their visors. All we need to do is tell them this one sentence, "**1,000 CD quality songs that fits in your pocket**," and everyone will understand the problem we fix. That one sentence alone made Apple the most valuable company to this day. To make Jobs offer even more impressive, the line, "**automatically downloads all your iTunes songs and playlists into your iPod**," was enough to win over everyone too busy with their own lives to worry about how to properly compress an MP3 file using an unfamiliar software.

Overall, Steve Jobs was a great leader because of his keen ability to understand the needs and the problems of his target audience and deliver that message in a way that the everyday person could easily digest. Same with Southwest Airlines and their "low-fare carrier" — everybody got it; no need for an explanation. If you want the cheapest tickets, call them.

In the early 80's, Domino's pizza figured out that all people cared about was speed. They didn't care about ordering Mama's homecooked sauce from Sicily; they didn't care how they just wanted the pizza as fast as possible. So, Domino's created their "**30-minute guarantee**" from the time an order is placed — or its free if it costs under $300. However, that message wouldn't resonate with someone who cared about the sauce, how the crust was made, and didn't care about how soon they got it — that message wouldn't work. But, they found that most of the time when people bought pizza, they wanted something quick and easy. Maybe they were watching the game or playing poker and wanted something as soon as possible for cheap.

Back to the business owner example: Let's assume you were working with a pizza owner back in those days and explained to them why the "30-minute guarantee" message works. If they failed to understand and started fighting you against it—then that's probably not a good customer to work with.

Become an Active Part of the Online Scene: Post Regularly and On a Trending Format Everyone's Using

Having an online brand is the way of the world now. That's why I decided to branch out further by using my techniques on myself. I began by observing what the people I want to talk about are posting on social media. From that, I determined that TV and radio are two platforms of consuming content that is fading into the background. Then I asked, "Well, what are they doing?" And found that they're watching YouTube videos, scrolling through Facebook, and listening to podcasts on their morning commute to work. I then decided to apply that knowledge to my own business. Now, I am the host of a live Facebook show and iTunes Podcast, "Think Like a Marketer Show." I also have another podcast called the, "Mind Theory Podcast," on iTunes.

Engage With Customers on Multiple Social Media Platforms

The main advantage I have over my competitors is that I understand the value of posting content on the internet that other people aren't willing to on a consistent basis. One of which is posting a live show on Facebook every week. In addition, I also know what to do with that live show content to make people to maximize its potential for engagement. That is to say, it's what I did with the live show afterward that perpetuated my brand to where it is today.

- **First:** I would cut around a one-minute chunk of content out where I said something provocative when I was interviewing a guest and post it on my Instagram.

- **Second:** I would take a 10-minute segment and put it on LinkedIn.

- **Third:** I would take the entire interview and send it to my Email list and say, "Hey, if you missed, check out my interview with a professional wrestler and he tells you something you didn't know about Hulk Hogan.

- **Fourth:** I would upload it to my YouTube channel, and try to get viewers to subscribe as they're watching the actual video.

- **Fifth:** I would upload the audio to a Podcast to be a part of the podcast field.

- **Lastly,** on certain shows—I would upload the transcript and turn it into a blog post for my website.

After completing each step, I've successfully marketed my Facebook live show on six different social media platforms — all from one live show. Even more, whether my viewers watch my show is irrelevant; the fact that they see it is enough for me. On top of that — most people I interview for my Facebook live show also have their own shows as well. So, when they come on as a guest for me, I'll say something like, "Hey, I'll be on your show as if you come on mine."

That is the difference between one brand and another brand: **One is simply talking more about themselves than the other**.

Practice Makes Perfect

My advice to entrepreneurs or business owners is to start their own live show and commit to posting once a week. At first, you won't have any clue what you're doing, and you'll feel like a fool. But — if you give it time, you'll start watching yourself and start to pick up on little things such as saying too many "likes" or "ums," when you talk. Eventually, you'll grow comfortable watching yourself; hearing yourself; and listening to your message that you naturally develop confidence the more you post. As you get comfortable talking and interacting with others on camera, when someone asks you to come on their live show, you won't even feel nervous anymore. You'll know exactly what you want to say, and you say it with confidence.

The biggest challenge I've encountered when it comes to digital marketing is something, I believe most business owners can resonate with: Coming to terms with reality and admitting that you don't know everything. And, that in order to run a successful business, you have to first rely on your ability to find the right people for your company who work together cohesively.

Bosses: Use PCAN Method for Bombarding Questions / Problems People Bring to Your Office

Early on, everyone would come to me with their problems—asking me what to do. Initially this made me feel competent because they view me as an authority figure. I would give them the answer and they'd leave. Well, as your organization grows, you can't have everybody coming to you to solve their problems; that's what you hired them to do. It wasn't until I read the book, "The Art of Woo," that they gave me the answer to this dilemma. The answer was: If someone comes into your office—use the PCAN Method which is an acronym for:

PROBLEM: Using this method, an employee would come into my office and tell me their problem.

CAUSE: Ask yourself, "What do you think the cause is?" Once you determine the cause, then answer, "The cause is XYZ."

ANSWER: Then I'll ask them, "What do you think the answer or the solution to that problem is?" And if they don't know, I tell them to go figure it out and come back with an answer.

NET-BENEFIT: How do we, the company, and the consumer benefit in the process?

Now, when employees come into my office with a problem you think I need to know about — have already prepared:

- What you think the cause is
- What you think the solution is
- How the company / client benefits

Which employee do you think is going to get promoted faster:

1. The employee that comes up to you and says, "Hey, we've got this problem. What should I do?
2. Or, the employee that says, "Hey, we've got this problem. I think the problem is xyz, but here I did a little research and I found out if we do this, it will increase our margins by 10%.

Difficult to decide? I don't think so. The answer: Ding! Ding! Ding! -employee number two gets promoted every time.

The Mantra I Run My Businesses' By

In conclusion, I'd like to share the mantra I've started and grown multiple successful companies from: **Good things come to those who wait. And it's only the things left over from the people who got there before you.** In laymen's terms — you better get a head start to get there to get the cookie because if you wait too long, all that's left is going to be crumbs from the people who got there before you. It's the people who are willing to jump through hoops and push through all the hard work faster than you that will inherit the riches. And, if you're still confused—here's an even simpler expression without all the fluff: Early bird gets the worm.

The people who get there first are those with courage; they were willing to act in spite of fear and do it anyway. They are the clients of mine who didn't feel comfortable being on camera but decided to do it anyway. And they started doing it and gradually grew confidence until others began noticing the benefit. Meanwhile, you're already way ahead of them and they have to run to catch up to your shadow. They can try to follow your footsteps and do all the stuff you did two years ago, but you're already way ahead of them.

Healthy Body, Healthy Mind with Kailee Wong

"Watch your thoughts; they become words.
Watch your words; they become actions.
Watch your actions; they become character.
Watch your character; it becomes your destiny."

- Lao Tzu

All of my life, I identified myself as an athlete. After years of hard work and practice, I was fortunate enough to achieve the pinnacle of my career success as an athlete when drafted as a starter in the NFL. During this time, I was blessed to play the sport that I loved and get paid for it. But, like gravity, what goes up must come down.

I'll be the first to admit—football is a dangerous game. When you watch your favorite pro-athletes on the field Sunday night, most don't take into account the hours of blood, sweat, and tears involved. Football players are like cars; the more they're hit, the more they dent.

When we're born, I believe we're all built for greatness. We're all born athletes because our bodies are designed for movement. But as we grow older, our bodies are pushed to their limits—some more than others. Though I took care of my body, it wasn't operating at its full potential the more I played in the NFL. On the team, I experienced several injuries: a patella tendon knee and an Achilles—both on the right side of my body.

Soon, the pain became intolerable and reached a breaking point. At that moment, I had to make a decision: either retire, or play a couple more years in the NFL and jeopardize my long-term mobility. Choosing option number two would mean sacrificing my ability to play with my children and my ability to travel with my wife. That wasn't going to happen. As a husband and father, my needs no longer come first, and my decision was final. I retired from the NFL.

Corporate America, Here I Come

Despite my dedication to football in college, I didn't slack off in the classroom. I was a diligent worker and graduated from the Stanford Hall of Fame class of 2018 with a degree in Economics. With a degree in hand, I was ready to hit the ground running and make myself known on Wall Street. Though stressful at times, I loved my job in the corporate America world. I was making *really* good money—I'm talking borderline pro-athlete money—and learning valuable skills and insight from other successful businessmen around me. Imagine operating on the same level as a bunch of A-type personalities in their mid-to-late thirties. Let's just say, the standards were high.

Coping with Pain at Work

One day, I'm sitting in my office and feel a pain in my lower back. Time progresses, and the pain slowly gets worse. My workouts weren't the same — what used to be very intense training now comprised of an hour on the elliptical machine. It drove me crazy because I identify myself as an athlete. At lunch one day, I ask some of my coworkers if they also deal with pain at work. I was active, working out regularly, in my early thirties, an ex-football player — things weren't adding up.

Here's what I found ...*every one* of the coworkers I spoke with — some never played a sport in their life — all agreed with a resounding "Of course!"

"This is what being thirty-five is like!" they all boomed in agreeance.

I didn't understand. "Do I have to choose between a high paying job and my physical wellbeing? Don't my coworkers want more from their lives?" I thought to myself. Or perhaps they just accepted it, not knowing that the option to have both was available. Either way, I wanted more for my life.

The Defining Moment That Changed My Life

One night, I was standing eating dinner while my wife and kids sat at the dinner table. Confused, my wife looked at me said, "What's wrong, babe? Sit down, come have dinner with us." And I replied, "I want to, baby, but my body hurts so bad. I can't even sit down."

I remember thinking to myself...*who am I?* Afterward, I spoke with my wife and told her about my idea for a new business I wanted to call "The Athletic Room." I said, "At the end of the day, it might not work. But if so, we're just going to have to move to New Mexico — or somewhere random, I'll teach the kids to hunt elk, and we'll live in a double-wide. Either way, this is something I have to do." And she said, "Alright, let's do it."

My wife and I know that **without your health, you have no wealth**.

The Prevalence of Lower Back Pain

Studies show that back pain is a significant health concern in Western countries — with an overwhelming **60%-80%** of adults reporting at least low levels of back pain. Back pain is the most prevalent musculoskeletal condition and correlated with an increase in medical expenditure and work absence.

It finally dawned on me...when I was playing football, I used my body as a tool to monetize. How is corporate America any different?

The answer is simple: when you're sitting at a desk, you don't *realize* that your body is a tool for making money because no one emphasizes its importance. You're there to perform a job well and leave.

The majority of higher-ups in corporate America don't understand how reduced mobility, dysfunction, and discomfort can dull brainpower. Let's take a top litigator, for example. Assume he's preparing for the top case to date in his career, and he's struggling with back pain. He has to sit in court for nine hours a day over three months. Imagine trying to focus on important issues when your body is in immense pain. That's a big issue.

Office Jobs & Musculoskeletal Pain

For those who don't know, football causes macro stress on the body; imagine running headfirst into a 300-pound guy repeatedly over a three-and-a-half-hour period. Sitting at a desk causes micro stress. Both cause harm to your physical health, just in different ways.

The #1 person prone to musculoskeletal issues is an office worker—more than those working in heavy construction or an oil field. **Our bodies are designed for movement, designed to move; only recently have we stopped moving.**

Office workers are the main target for musculoskeletal pain. Inactivity is the root cause of their sickness and dysfunction, because a sedentary lifestyle starves your muscles of the movement necessary to operate over time. When we sit in a cubicle—inactive for eight hours every day—our bodies are quite literally attacking themselves on the inside.

Repetitive movements, whether it's someone who's an avid runner or a cyclist, those continual movements cause stress to your body, which will eventually cause dysfunction.

The Idea Behind The Athletic Room

Initially, I got into this field of work from my past and my love for acupuncture, massage, cold therapy, heat therapy, and all the other forms of recovery therapy pro athletes become accustomed to over the years. However, to receive each of those treatments, I had to go to multiple places; it wasn't convenient. For this reason, I wanted to create a multi-purpose facility that treats various health and recovery issues at once.

The Athletic Room provides a range of elite-level services to the everyday person that are typically only given to top athletes. My #1 goal is to help every person who walks through the door to feel and move their best.

Our team at The Athletic Room creates an environment of comfort for our clients. We do this by gathering a team of smart, certified, and knowledgeable, trained professionals who know what they're talking about and are ready to educate our clients. Each team member can speak endlessly about body maintenance and proper recovery — which is something so unique from any other place offering regenerative medicine treatment.

7 Ways to Care for Your Health

1. Prioritize Recovery

Here at The Athletic Room, we help our clients in three core areas of recovery:

1. Maintenance & Improve Flexibility
2. Address & Reduce Systemic Inflammation
3. Circulation & Blood Flow

A little bit about me: My Dad played college football—could've played pro football but went to Vietnam because he was in ROTC in High School. Nonetheless, listening to his stories over the years—to rest and recover meant to be weak. He didn't invest in the recovery aspect of fitness and health. Today, I understand that recovery is a process and the reason behind the exercise benefits we love to see. Without recovery, you're robbing your body of its ability to heal and grow back stronger.

According to Merriam-Webster, the medical definition of the principle General Adaptation is the following: the sequence of physiological reactions to prolonged stress in the classification of Hans Selye includes alarm, resistance, and exhaustion. In essence, the reason we put our bodies under stress (through an intense workout or lifting heavy weights) is to allow it to grow back and adapt to the volume, so that the next time, you can train just a little bit harder with ease. Recovery is simply the time between training sessions that *allows* your body to grow and come back stronger.

For example, let's say you're watching your favorite team on Sunday night football, and DeAndre Hopkins takes a hard hit and limps off the field. You may get super worried and say, "Aw, man! Next week's a big game; we need him! He's our best wide receiver." But then, all of a sudden, next Sunday rolls around, and Hopkins is out on the field, running routes, catching every pass, and is as good as you've ever seen him.

How did that happen? You may think it's because he's this miracle healer...but is he? It's more likely that his body is optimized to allow it to heal itself fast from years of investing in the recovery of his body.

2. Listen to Your Body

> *"When your body whispers at you, there's a lot that you can do for it. But, once it starts screaming, your options are a lot less."*
>
> *– Kailee Wong*

The Athletic Room isn't doing anything crazy; we're merely encouraging our clients to invest time and energy to keep your body moving the way it's designed to move. Your body is smarter than all of us recognize, so why not allow it to heal itself by optimizing the state that it's in to repair the way it was made?

An example is one of the top physicians here in Houston and someone on our advisory board at The Athletic Room — Dr. Mark Adickes. He told me this: "The reason why I'm so behind what you're doing is that **60%** of the people that come in to see me that we *have* to operate on didn't have to get here. The reason we couldn't wait is because they failed to address their pain for so long that now, there's no option but perform surgery."

Again, it goes back to this idea:

> *"If your body is whispering at you — you have a lot of different avenues you can take to heal. But, once it starts*

screaming at you — there are limited remedies available to you."

Adickes stated, "These patients could've prevented this if they would've just done *something* — whether that something is acupuncture, chiropractic care, pilates, stretching, yoga, etc."

4. Eat Healthy to Counteract Inflammation

Chronic inflammation is the reason why **90%** of the people go to the ER and one of the top causes of death. Think of cancer, depression, heart disease — all are caused by chronic inflammation. One of the largest culprits of inflammation in America is our unhealthy diet. In 2016, the British Medical Journal found that **80%** of the calories from American diets come from ultra-processed foods. If you fall into that category, that means calorically, **21.6%** of your calories come from added sugars.

Compare that to the standard diet of the 1800s. During that time, humans would consume — over five days — the amount of sugary food equivalent to a standard can of soda. Now, we consume that volume every seven hours! And the research shows that with more sugar comes more inflammation.

5. Improve Flexibility & Mobility

Studies have shown that introducing flexibility post-operation improves healing time by up to **50%**. There are also studies analyzing performance for golfers who introduced stretching routines into their golf games against a group that didn't add them increased their accuracy by 23% and increased their total drive distance by 17 yards.

We have people who stretch to help with balance because once you get over 70, it is critical because a lack of balance is one of the leading causes of natural death. The outlook of life-expectancy isn't favorable after you fall and hit your head or break a hip. So, we see our client's balance scores increase because they have a better range of motion and better flexibility.

6. Don't Become Sedentary

Body maintenance means your body can withhold its original design. We all remember how easy it was as a kid to do a bear crawl, or touch your toes, or be in happy baby pose. It not only feels good, but it's playful. As we grow up, we, for some reason, adopt the false notion that this is how it is because I'm older. My belief? It doesn't have to be that way. Sure, as you age, your body's mobility naturally declines due to changes, but you expedite the process when sedentary.

Your body changes due to the way you interact with your environment.

There was a study done in Australia examining the way kindergarteners move and run during recess. From observation, they found that almost all kindergarteners had impeccable form. After second grade, the researchers re-evaluated the same group. The results show that instead of running mid-foot strikers (the ideal running posture based on the ideal body mechanics), up to 3/4ths of them transitioned to heel-strike runners. This type of running is not suitable because you slow yourself down every time you strike your heel first. Intrigued by the findings, the researchers wanted to understand the reason *why* this adjustment happened.

The researchers found that in kindergarten, you're exposed to a much more active, Montessori-like environment. You sit on the floor crisscross applesauce, you read on the floor, you're moving regularly. In contrast, second graders sit in a desk almost all day.

When you sit in a desk all day, your body-mechanics start to conform to the posture you're putting it in repeatedly. This changes how your body responds to its environment. When you sit, your diaphragm compresses. If you notice, as we age, we start to become chest breathers when we used to be belly breathers.

When you breathe from your chest, this puts excess stress and disengages your psoas. The psoas is the strongest muscle in your body responsible for creating hip extensions and inflections — the psoas powers the glutes powered by the hip flexors. In a seated position, you shorten your hip flexors. **If you sit for extended periods — your hip flexors will shrink as they adapt to the situation.** Your body is always looking for ways to be at rest; to enter homeostasis. The act of something repetitive naturally changes your gait, and your body adapts to its environment.

#7 Lift Weights

Before, we talked about how I was relegated to an elliptical and grinding away in corporate America. Now, five years later—I run, compete in Brazilian jiu-jitsu, lift weights, practice yoga, go on hikes, cycle, and so on.

In short, that's the idea of the body; we're designed to adapt and perform a lot of different movements frequently.

As far as exercise is concerned, I've found lifting weights to be one of the best anti-aging activities for both males and females. Lifting weights also increases the body's testosterone levels, and, though many don't realize, testosterone is equally as crucial for women as it is for men.

In college, you might go to the gym, aiming to burn about 500 calories. Most hop on the elliptical or treadmill and do cardio to burn 500 calories—which is lovely. However, the moment you stop moving, your body stops burning calories. When you lift weights, your resting metabolic rate increases, so the afterburn of lifting weights is where the real benefits reside. While during that hour of weightlifting, you may not have burned as much as cardio, the aftereffect of the increase in your resting metabolic rate is night and day difference from only doing cardio.

Social Media Rules for 2020

#1 Post Consistently

At The Athletic Room, for every shift our athlete advisors take, they are required to post two stories on Instagram for two reasons:

1. To increase our social media engagement.

2. So others can understand the stories of our athletes and how our services help their issues.

For example, one of our clients had a dream to run around the world. To accomplish this, she ran multiple marathons: One along the Great Wall of China, another amongst the castles in Scotland, another in Chicago, and more. She has a phenomenal story. Had we not been so adamant about posting stories every shift, we might not have even known about why she was using our services.

#2 Share Stories Worth Hearing

Each time a client shares a story on our Instagram page, it increases engagement. Whether it's their going to Dubai to compete in a Jiu-Jitsu tournament or training for their first triathlon in Galveston — whatever it is, that's a great story that should be turned into content to share with the world. The whole premise of social media activity is to share new information consistently.

How to Achieve Happiness

I'm a big proponent of teaching happiness because I believe the world starts with how you perceive a situation, moment, or challenge in life.

"How you experience life depends on how you perceive it."

-Kailee Wong

For me, the secret to happiness is picking the right spouse. I am lucky and blessed to have chosen the right person and that she picked me. It's so calming to know that whatever happens—we're solid. After that, it's what you feed your mind.

I'll end this chapter with a story:

One day, a grandfather is sitting in the woods with his grandson. They are observing a white wolf and a black wolf attacking each other in front of them. The grandfather turns to the grandson and asks, "Which wolf do you think will win?" Assuming each wolf is equally as strong and fierce as the other and the white representing 'good' and the black representing 'evil.' The son replies, "I don't know, grandad." The grandfather replies, "The one that's going to win is the one you feed most."

The moral of this story is this: **what you feed your mind is what will take place in your world**. The saying is true—we end up believing the lies that we tell ourselves. For example, if you always think, "I'm not good enough," in your head, you reaffirm that thought in your brain, and your actions will follow suit to fit that narrative.

How to Turn Adversity into Success with The LinkedIn Authority with Freddy Goerges

Back in 2012, I started an organization called Houston Young Professionals on LinkedIn. It quickly grew to over 27 thousand followers. Now, it is the largest networking organization on LinkedIn.

I call myself the "LinkedIn Authority" because I teach employers, professionals, and brands how to grow their business using LinkedIn strategies and other third-party tools. I show my clients how to incorporate LinkedIn as a marketing tool to connect and engage with their audience and foster new relationships.

What Makes Someone an "Expert" Authority

The difference between an average person and an expert authority figure online boils down to what they're willing to go through to master their chosen platform. For example, how much time will you take to learn the ins-and-outs of Linkedin—from advertising to marketing to networking with peers? Once you reach a certain level as a professional, the next step to becoming an expert is to differentiate yourself from the crowd. Attaining authority is a challenge because the internet never sleeps. Every day, there's someone new calling themselves an expert online.

If you have 1,000 people calling themselves the "expert," how do you stand out amongst the crowd?

It's for this reason that I decided to label myself as "The Linkedin Authority," as opposed to other, more generic names others have given themselves. Here are three ways to stand out as an authoritative business figure:

#1 Discover Your Target Audience

Once you narrow down your particular niche and platform to become an authority figure, the next step is to locate your target audience.

The author of *Build Your Brand Mania*, Matt Bertram, tells young entrepreneurs, "Show the power of knowing your target market's problems and then [create] content to meet a specific need they [have] (93)." "By getting inside your customer's head, you will understand the kind of problems they have and can offer solutions they are looking for, and you will be able to build content that will talk directly to them and their needs," he explained (92).

If you're still having a hard time pinpointing your target audience, here are some helpful questions to get the ball rolling:

1. What motivates my audience?
2. What is the desired action of my target audience?
3. What are their fears, and how can I help lessen those fears?
4. How does my brand help them reach their goal?
5. What demographic groups would take the desired action?

#2 Become a Problem Solver

When it comes to problem-solving, ignorance is your enemy. You want to discover your client's problem as soon as possible. One tried-and-true way to address this right out the gate is to set up an initial consultation to get to know your customer.

For example, the majority of my clients come to me to find methods and strategies to increase revenue for their business. I always start with a one-on-one personal approach to meet with them and start by pulling the layers back one at a time. To begin, I ask them what their goals and objectives are for increasing business revenue. Then, I show them the Linkedin strategies, ideas, and tools to help their unique situation.

#3 Adopt Consultative-Approach

The purpose of a consultant-approach is to get your clients to open up and share their stories. This will help them to view the interaction as building relationship activity as opposed to a shallow transaction. If you successfully get your client to share their story, you'll typically find a few golden nuggets that you can emphasize or highlight. Use these nuggets to help narrow down who their target audience is and determine their subsequent needs, wants, and fears as a person and brand.

One thing that I advise is to treat a business as a ministry, or an opportunity to be the witness in front of them without being on the pulpit preaching to them. I use this analogy to use the time I have with my clients as an opportunity to engage, share ideas, and openly discuss any questions, comments, or concerns they may have. Often, after I've sat down with a client and used this approach, I discover that they are struggling with more than generating business. Marital issues, conflict with a coworker or even themselves are what's holding them back from reaching their full potential.

My first hour of LinkedIn workshops is always dedicated to learning more about my client's product, service, what sets them apart from their competitors, and so on. From experience, clients particularly benefit from the consultant approach the most because all they truly want is someone who's going to be there to listen to help them recognize other issues they are facing, yet not necessarily verbalizing at the time.

LinkedIn Rules For 2020

#1 Complete Your LinkedIn Profile

If you don't complete your profile on LinkedIn, you are showing potential employers or people interested in working with you that you are NOT their ideal candidate. How could you be if you couldn't even put in the effort to flesh out a well thought out Linkedin profile?

Talk is cheap, *especially* on Linkedin.

You may claim to be the best Realtor in the state of Texas or a five-time award-winning salesperson in the oil and gas field. But at the end of the day—if your words and actions don't line up—it will make others question your integrity.

Remember this: Always provide evidence! If you won an award, link it to your profile. If you're a writer, attach a portfolio of your work for others to view. If you were a top-performing salesman at your last company, don't just leave it at that—include proof such as "Improved territory sales from $5 million to $7 million within a year and a half."

#2 Think Outside the Box

One of the biggest misconceptions I hear is that Linkedin is a job board or somewhere to hang your resume. If I'm a potential customer or client wanting to learn more about you—a resume and job description isn't going to be enough to convince me of your competency.

For me to give you at least five minutes of my time for a phone conversation or face-to-face meeting, I'd want to see more than the basics. Think creatively! LinkedIn is a great platform to provide evidence of your competency by attaching video testimonials, PowerPoints, case studies, white papers, marketing brochures, and more attached as a PDF. Think of it as a way to sell yourself on a one-page landing page or website.

#3 Post Regularly

Whenever you look at social media now, most people are consuming their content — whether that be movies, podcasts, music, etc. — through their smartphones. What happens over time if your profile has a high frequency of activity is that your followers see your picture floating around all this time. From what I've seen, this creates somewhat of a 'presumed celebrity status.' Because you post so regularly, your followers will naturally assume that you must be doing everything right.

I know that everyone won't see or read every piece of content I post, but they're going to be familiar enough with me to where they feel like they know me as a human being. With Linkedin, one thing that I do that I've found builds people's trust is that I'm not afraid to wear my faith on my sleeve. I share inspirational and faithful quotes that tell people who I am on the inside as a person. Humbleness is enough to allow others to feel comfortable to open up in return. For me, when I can connect with someone else as my authentically true self, that's what builds my trust.

#4 Share Your Story

Your story is so compelling because once your audience learns your story, they see more than just your success. Initially, they may think you are a 'one-hit-wonder' or were lucky enough to be blessed from the beginning and given things too easily. For this reason, it's paramount to build the foundation of everything you had to overcome to achieve the success you have today.

My Story

In 2008, I received my first LinkedIn invitation and had recently started a new job in business development. When I got my first LinkedIn request, I saw the opportunity available, knowing that all of my target audience of HR and business managers were active on LinkedIn. One of my job functions at the time was too cold call or cold visit employers to talk to their HR and benefits managers about our wellness program, executive health program, and drug screening programs.

Like most, cold calling wasn't exactly my forte. So, to make it easier, I decided to create a LinkedIn group for HR and benefits managers. Low and behold, within a year, over 1,000 people followed the group. At that moment, a lightbulb went off in my head about just how monumental LinkedIn could be one day for my career.

Hitting Rock Bottom

Fast forward to 2008, and I was going through a divorce, and the world was in financial turmoil due to the financial crisis. I found myself in a low spot in my life as I was experiencing financial difficulties and marital difficulties and had every reason to be depressed. My income nearly dropped in half. After a year of hard work, my boss gave me a 20% raise—which is rare in the corporate world.

Now, here are five tips I wish I had when I was at my worst:

#1 Use Time to Your Advantage

"If you have more money than you have time, hire someone else to do it, but if you have more time than money, invest your time, and do it yourself."

–Co-Founder of Direct Response Marketing Agency—Spoken About, Randall Chesnutt

When I was struggling financially and maritally, I had an abundance of time on my hands. Long story short, I was bored, lonely, and depressed. I often was awake through the night and began to connect with people on LinkedIn.

Before my life took a turn for the worse, I didn't have a network. I believed the false narrative of "The American Dream" that teaches us the same script to success. All you have to do is go to High School, graduate college, get a good job, find a wife and kids—and the rest will fall magically into place. My American Dream seemed more like an American Nightmare as if my world had closed down. It was as if a dark cloud loomed over my head constantly. In an attempt to escape that darkness, I poured everything leftover into my career.

#2 Build Your Network

"Loneliness is the enemy's playground."

– Freddy Goerges

2012 rolled around, and at the time, I would've called myself a new professional or expert on LinkedIn, but I was looking for social growth. I was recently divorced, and men and women aren't built for isolation; we are social creatures. For a while, I tried to attain a leadership position at some other young professional groups. With newfound courage, I decided to become the leader of my own path and start my own networking group on LinkedIn — and here we are today!

Within the first month, I booked over 1,000 people when it took me a year with HR and benefits managers, because these young professionals are hungry for community. Hope fosters when you can look forward to meeting someone new or having an exciting and engaging conversation in your head. Without that sense of connection, how can you build or grow your own stable sphere of influence?

#3 Be a Leader, Not a Follower

As someone who understands human behavior well, most people either want to be the leader or want to be next to the leader. I chose to take the initiative to lead; I was willing to take that risk. I could've failed, but I was so consistent, one competitor said that I was on a "warpath." After reflection, one could say that my intense drive and consistency was a way for me to occupy my mind, which was battling lonely and depressed thoughts. It's not that I necessarily believe in astrology, but I believe in the God that created the stars, and perhaps he created patterns during those astrological times.

#4 Control Your Mindset

My life philosophy: Control your emotions, or your emotions will control you.

Growing up, I was the shyest kid in school. I stuttered so badly people thought I had a learning disability. I was the youngest of four and had jacked-up teeth because we couldn't afford braces, and the clothes I wore were hand-me-downs from the garage sale. **Long story short, the experiences around me were building a mindset of limitation and self-doubt.**

Back then, I could count all my friends on one hand, and instead of wallowing in self-pity, I began to shift my negative energy into positive by focusing on self-development self-growth. It all came down to me grasping the idea that if I don't have a community around me, then I'm not going to have any resources to lean on. I'm not going to have wise counsel to counsel me, I won't have anyone to ask a favor for, or anyone to derive new ideas or directions for whatever I'm going through.

#5 Turn Your Weaknesses into Strengths

I'm incredibly emotional, empathetic, and intuitive. And that type of person is like a radio transformer — if they don't pay attention to what frequency they're sending out or picking up, then there's a lot of lousy junk that that will pour into them. So, instead of cowering in defeat and letting the dark cloud consume me, I instead decided to make good of all of my talents and use them to help out those struggling who need help. I give the members of the Houston Networking Professionals network a time and a day to meet up for a shared sense of community.

A Parting Word:

My point in sharing my story is not to give off the impression that I'm still depressed or stuck in that negative space in the present day. The reason why I share my story is to exemplify how sometimes crisis, failure, depression, or other overwhelming life circumstances can lead to good if you invest your time for good. Without my past, it wouldn't have led to this brand—instead, shall I say—a community of Houston Young Professionals.

Create Shock Value and Prove Your Naysayers Wrong with Taylor Waidhofer

"Set yourself on fire, and people will gather to watch you burn."

– Taylor Waidhofer

To be an entrepreneur, you must first rise above the expectations of others. You must go all-in—leaving no room for "what-ifs" that may linger in your mind otherwise. This determination toward a higher purpose requires laser-like focus, grit, and most of all—thick skin that only the 1% hold within.

I'd like to dedicate this chapter to everyone who said I *couldn't*. Here's the story of how I *did*.

I'll split this chapter into three sections: my background, my business, and my advice. I hope this encourages aspiring entrepreneurs like yourself to remain true to yourself and never let others' opinions dictate your life choices.

My Background

I'm a native Houstonian. I lived in Austin for four years while trying out for different pro-ice hockey teams. However, through trial and error, I quit hockey and came back to Houston. I attended Blinn Community College and Houston community college, totaling about a year before deciding to drop out and pursue real estate full time.

Nine years ago, I started my first entrepreneurial business venture: a corporate gifting business in the real estate industry. This gifting business engraved personalized gifts that targeted realtors, lenders, and builders called ClutchCity Gifts. Starting ClutchCity Gifts invited me into the real estate community, making it relatively easy to launch the company I run now.

Building My Brand Online

Once social media marketing became popular, I took full advantage. I started running around like a chicken with my head cut off, taking selfies with me in every real estate office in the city to promote my new business. I would pitch my business in front of a group of agents like RE/MAX, Paul Baker, and Telebaker, to make connections with the top real estate agents in Houston. Over seven years, I must have presented over 1,000 times—taking pictures to post online along the way.

My online following started primarily on Facebook. But the bulk of my audience came from me going out and presenting in front of the best real estate agents in Houston. I leveraged primarily email marketing, Facebook posts, and video content.

To make this possible, I host a popular podcast and YouTube show called **Disruption Nation**, where I put people on blast that are disrupting the space in a positive way in and outside the real estate community. For my podcast, we do what's called a "daily disruption," where every day, I make a 30-40 second video to post on Facebook. To date, I've done over 300 of them and counting.

Disruption Nation features some of the best agents in the city. I've also had judges, salvation army generals, the president of the downtown Houston rotary club, and other prominent Houston CEOs.

My Business

I am the owner and publisher of **Houston Real Producers Magazine**, which is a monthly magazine that connects businesses with the top 1% residential realtors in the greater Houston area. Established in 2017, the Houston Real Producers Magazine is a private trade magazine for the top 500 realtors in the Houston market. To this day, Houston Real Producers continues to help local real estate agents connect with top businesses across Houston.

In addition to my podcast, **Disruption Nation**, I host monthly educational events with panels exclusive for the staff agents and advertising partners in the city that fund our business. During these events, keynote speakers add value through shared knowledge to the real estate community called **Masterclass Houston**. So far, we've partnered with over 75 of the best businesses. Our audience closed a minimum of $17 million last year, led to over 25,000 transactions, and over 10 million dollars in closed business.

OUTCOME

We want to be known as master connectors in the real estate community and as a company that adds a tremendous amount of value to the industry. The realtors don't pay a dime for the content we produce in Houston Real Producers magazine; it's all about them and helping others.

CLIENT MISCONCEPTIONS

The biggest client misconception is trust because they think print advertising is old news and not going to add value to their business. Yet, our company gains the majority of the ROI and revenue from referrals and relationships. What I tell people is we're a relationship-building platform. It is 100% about the quality of relationships you will form through attending the Monthly Mastermind panels, quarterly social events, summer boat parties, and listening to the guests on Disruption Nation. The Houston Real Producers magazine is used only as glue to connect people further online to build a better relationship. In other words, I use social media platforms to get people together so that our relationships can evolve. It's so much more than just print.

TOP BENEFITS

- Introductions to some of the best people in the real estate market that aren't easily accessible otherwise.

- A platform where you can build relationships with top-ranking industry professionals in real estate.

- Streamline your business growth by connecting with the best real estate agents in the city with lots of network connections.

Q: SO, YOU GUYS ARE KIND OF LIKE REALTORS, EXCEPT YOU HELP GET PEOPLE CONNECTIONS/REFERRALS?

We support the realtor. We cater to realtors because everything we do is free for them. The realtors benefit from the value that we provide. For example, on average, a realtor would have to pay $10,000-$15,000 for what I do for them for free. We build them up all over the city visually and in print, and they don't have to pay a cent for our service because it's funded by lenders, roofers, warranty, food companies, contractors, factories, painters, you name it. Additionally, the events/parties we hold are private and exclusive, so when we have one, everybody I just listed off gets invited: the best agents in the city and all those businesses. All you pay is a monthly fee as part of an advertising partnership with Houston Real Producers.

My Advice

#1. Find a Mentor

"Be bold and mighty forces will come to your aid."

– Grant Cardone

Finding a mentor is a significant first step for any up-and-coming entrepreneur looing to "learn the ropes." This is where having a broad network comes in handy because you never know who your friend, family member, or friend-of-a-friend may know that has the ideal career you aspire to achieve. If you don't have someone specific in mind, utilize the power of LinkedIn to reach out to people in business and ask for the chance to start with an internship or even request to work 60 days free to show your dedication depending on your financial circumstances.

Throughout my journey as an entrepreneur, I found my mentor online. For me, Grant Cardone taught me to:

- Adopt an unbreakable mindset positive
- Never quit
- Adopt a do-it mentality
- Be a fireman — to put out fires rather than start them
- Outwork and outlast the competition.

"If we each get on a treadmill right now, one of two things are going to happen…either you're going to get off first, or I am going to die. Period."

– **Will Smith**

#2. There Are No Shortcuts

"Insanity is doing the same thing over and over again and expecting different results."

-**Albert Einstein**

Many people hold the false notion that running a successful business comes with finding the "shortcut" or silver-bullet to success. It's my job to help people understand that anything in life worth having takes hard work.

For example, it's like signing up for a gym membership. If you utilize the membership and consistently work on your fitness goals, you'll get the most out of it. But, if you sign up in January, but continue to slack off and eat junk food for six months, chances are your body will respond accordingly.

A weak mindset is probably the biggest problem I have when working with clients. I can give them all the tools, advice, and guidance to succeed, but it's ultimately their choice whether to participate, show-up, or engage with the people that I've connected them with.

In other words: You can lead a horse to water, but you can't make him drink.

#3. Figure Out What Success Means To You

For me, success means the legacy that you're able to leave through your work. And what motivates me, or what I'd refer to as my "claim to fame," is that I am a full-time single father. I've been a single father since my boys were one and three years old. Now, they're seven and nine. I'm writing a book right now called "**Shock Value.**" The book is about my life story and the power of using shock value in either a negative or positive way.

In my case, I was blindsided with a negative shock value. I believed that I was going to be happily married forever and have a family unit. Then, boom—a lot of negatives started happening in my life that shattered those expectations. The overarching moral to my book is to help others bounce back and rise above challenging adversities they positively encounter throughout their life. I'm merely using my story as a basis to share how I rose above the dark times of my life.

#4. Be a Visionary, Hire Implementers

In my opinion, great leaders are visionaries. They come with an extraordinary level of enthusiasm and are great at finding the implementers to make their visions come to life. In other words, the visionaries would be the truck drivers that decide which direction to turn, while the implementers are ones who help turn the wheel to make it happen.

When I first became an entrepreneur, I tried to be both an implementer and visionary, but quickly failed because there's only so much time in the day. Now, we need a crew of talented and multi-faced individuals to help us implement different aspects of our company to help streamline our business success. Not everybody is like me—that's where the importance of building a team comes into play.

I've got a great team of office managers, publishing assistants, writers, photographers, videographers, Houston Real Producers advisory board, and more. There's a whole group of hard-working, passionate people backing what I do; I'm merely the face of the company.

#5. Be Better Than Your Naysayers

> *"Watch out for your naysayers—which is completely different than your haters."*
>
> -Taylor Waidhofer

Haters are easy to peg—their motto is: "You suck, you're not going to do well, and I can't wait to watch you fail." Naysayers, on the other hand, are more evil and dangerous, because you can't see them coming. They're often your family, friends, and loved ones; those who care about you the most and genuinely want to see you succeed.

However, at the same time, they're your biggest enemies. They'll tell you stories that confirm their own internal limiting beliefs like, "Yeah, I understand your dream, but you know what? I had this friend Mark, and he tried to do something similar and failed miserably, and I don't want to see you go through the same heartache." So, they'll inadvertently talk you out of pursuing your goals and dreams because they love and care about you. With this in mind, if you want something, don't listen to your naysayers. It will feel a bit unnatural at first, but you have to be very careful and private with your goals. Otherwise, the naysayers will throw sand on your fire when you're doing everything in your power to preserve it.

If you're struggling with feeling defeated by the naysayers around you, the primary way to overcome that fear is to prove them wrong over and over again until they no longer have any questions. After a while, if you do what you say and continually succeed — their questions will subside. One way to get them on your side is to say something like, "Look, I'm going through something tough right now, and I need your support on this situation that I'm working on." Other than that, keep your eyes on the prize until it's your reality.

Growth Strategies to Scale your Business in the Digital Era with Sami Khaleeq

Let's assume you're a supermodel on Instagram. Can you call yourself a supermodel tomorrow if Instagram shuts down?

Nowadays, if you're **not** on social media, you are going to be a dead business soon. I remember a time when people were saying that about a brick-and-mortar business without a website, and it was true! It's scary to think about how prevalent social media has become in the business world. And, the best way to remain afloat, is to use social media platforms as a marketing tool to boost clicks, engagement, and traffic to your company website.

When done correctly, this will increase engagement and sales inevitably. I always tell people to focus on not just the social media platforms themselves — instead, building a database of emails, as well as an optimized website for traffic. You never know what platform is going to come and go — take Vine, for example.

We live in an era where you cannot have a single-platform centric mindset when it comes to growing your business. Instead, social media platforms such as Instagram, Youtube, Facebook, Twitter, TikTok, are best used to drive traffic back to your website and boost audience engagement. Think omnipresence!

Q: WHEN CLIENTS COME TO YOU WHAT IS THEIR MAIN GOAL?

Clients come in looking for a multitude of outcomes. A few of the most common are:

- Grow Revenue
- Becoming a Industry Authority
- Increase Brand Awareness & Engagement

My Business

CGS Digital Marketing is a full-service web design and digital marketing agency where we equip our clients with strategies and creative solutions that deliver results. Our focus is to make you stand out in the digital space. We do branding and strategy that can be used in the legacy platforms, but we prefer making sure our clients are ready for today and tomorrow, not yesterday.

Our bread and butter is heavy compliance industries such as Healthcare, Financial Institutions, Law Firms and Government Agencies—just to name a few. Our team specializes in developing strategies. We pull big data from different vertices and find overlaps to apply it towards other industries. We develop skill sets and compliance heavy workflows that move seamlessly from healthcare to government-facing projects. We also study the demographics and locality of the business. Online, as with brick and mortar businesses, client persona is a big thing -- building their demographics is a crucial component of what we do.

Overall, our strategy focuses on questions such as:

1. Goal for using social media? Awareness? Sales? Loyalty and Retention?

2. Who is the Audience and What are Competitors doing online?

3. What does success of the project look like?

We often see that strategy is something many small businesses and entrepreneurs overlook. Because we saw this need in the market, we study strategy for our clients so they don't have to. Our strategic philosophy overall is to seek balance. We don't seek a single platform solution but what is proven to work time and time again as well as testing new things to stay on the cutting edge.

My Start

Most people don't expect it when they meet me, but before I got my break into digital marketing, I worked in cybersecurity. In the world of cybersecurity and information technology, ethical hacking was something that taught me the importance of **working within constraints, and that technology was only as smart as its user**. In some of the scenarios, companies would retain us to test the strength and flaws of their infrastructure and system. In doing so, it required us to study their system to interview their IT teams to figure out what kind of defects or weaknesses they may have brought to the team. This taught me social engineering strategies that become the bread-and-butter of marketing. I think the concept of hacking gets blurred with how Hollywood movies depict it because people don't realize that hackers are consuming a lot of research, analytical data, and studying human psychology and using that to perform a task and accomplish a mission.

My job as a cyber security consultant was to take an existing client system and maximize their security within the technology and with the tools they owned. Now we use a similar methodology when we build digital media strategies for clients. Strategies that help them reach their audience within the platforms they are marketing themselves in.

Some of my Top Strategies

When I look back at what helped me achieve success in scaling my agency there are a few things I can point to specifically.

1. Education, Education, Education

The day I stop looking for learning opportunities is the day they release my obituary." Education is an essential in life and in the industry. We invest time into our client's industries, and their companies when we take them on. We look for opportunities to increase the ROI by researching things that isn't just fluff from a hasty google search. Our goal is to be knowledgeable enough to educate the client on how the tools work, because we know that they will always be the expert in their industry. With this in mind, we do our research into their field so that we can have a conversation and research into the current events in industry to build strategy so that they don't have to educate us; but we can get into the strategy building with some speed.

Educating our clients is vital to earning their trust. To build trust and rapport with our clients, we consult with them and share market research on what they should be doing to be successful. My peers that work with other agencies often question why we're not speeding the sales process up within our agency, to this I always tell them,

> "The more we educate our clients, the more likely they'll turn into a trusted long-term client with us."

In short, what differentiates us the most is how much time we spend educating our clients. I think the biggest misunderstanding when it comes to social media is the belief that the best use of a social presence is to promote "sale, sale, sale". Instead, a successful social media user will focus on priorities like:

1. Listening

2. Educating their audience

3. Gaining trust and establishing themselves as an authority in their industry

4. Building a long-term relationship, or customer loyalty

People fail to realize that when you're in a "sale, sale, sale" mindset, it's not going to work effectively. Educating the client is a crucial element toward success whether it's through regularly posting informational podcasts, blog posts, or individually sitting with clients and educating them about your services, and only spending 10-20% of your time trying to sell or pitch.

2. Value Attitude Over Skill-Set

Many entrepreneurs wonder how to find the right people that will serve as valuable assets as part of their team. For me, I accomplished this by first becoming self-aware and determining my strengths and weaknesses and finding the areas where I needed outside help. This was another area where my cybersecurity background helped because it taught me how to read analytics, and present conformities and how to break them or improve them.

"You don't hire for skill; you hire for attitude."

- Simon Sinek

If you're currently an aspiring entrepreneur or small business owner looking to build a powerful team, I would advise you to prioritize attitude over skills, as skills can be taught. Still, it's much more challenging to alter someone's attitude. When I was finding the right people for my team, I hired people potential growth, not because of past performances. Easier to teach someone the first time than retrain them the second. I know that you can teach most people skills if they're willing to put in the work, so a great work ethic was something I prioritized in hiring. In addition to a great work ethic, I looked for people with an ability to perform consistently.

Aside from these two requirements, my ideal team members had little in common. I hired folks of all backgrounds — employees with a master's in mathematics, and Content Writers with a background in science. If I could tell that they were curious, adopted a willingness-to-learn attitude, and were eager to put the work in to master a skill, that's all I needed to know.

"Work like there is someone working 24 hours a day to take it away from you." **-Mark Cuban**

If you're trying to scale a business that's worth anything, working a 9-5 simply won't cut it. With this in mind, I caution young entrepreneurs against hiring based solely off of a fancy resume and impressive accolades if your team doesn't have the same vision as you, they won't be as driven to the same success as you.

3. Value Client Trust Over a Cheap Sale

We encounter a lot of burned clients—clients who've gone to either freelancers, overseas agencies, or local un-reputable agencies, and have had an investment with only loss, or burned as we say in the industry. These clients often don't trust us outright, which is understandable. For this reason, we make it a priority to spend some extra time gaining their trust and building a rapport with them. This requires a high level of patience that a lot of agencies simply don't factor into their timelines. Typically in this industry, when a client admits their hesitancy or distrust about the process, agencies will think, "Okay, this guy doesn't trust us," and move on to the next. But, for us, we're good at building that trust to turn new burnt clients into lifelong ones.

The sad reality of this situation is that there are many unethical and shady agencies and freelancers that burn others for short-term monetary gain. Rather than adopting a long-term goal and focusing on building, they prioritize landing "quick sales," only to disappear once they've cashed their check and burned a reputation to the ground.

4. There is No "Quick-Fix" to Grow Your Business Overnight

Even with top-notch strategies and social media tools, nothing lifechanging is going to happen in one or two weeks. You have to educate, research, and give genuine value to your customers to increase ROI. When you invest in your clients, it's a mutual gain. People forget that anything worth doing takes time. You have to invest and make it clear to the client that growth will take weeks and months, not hours and days to start seeing returns.

Final Thoughts

Our process is something that we feel is beneficial to all involved parties. And while sometimes we feel like we're not the right fit for a prospective client, we're not afraid to acknowledge that it isn't a perfect match, and refer them to a firm or individual who can help them meet their goals. Even if a company decides not to sign with us, it's part of our mission to go the extra mile and help them find the right agency that does have the tools and skills necessary to help them grow.

Q: WHAT ARE SOME INSTANCES WHERE YOU WOULDN'T BE ABLE TO HELP A CLIENT?

A couple of times that we felt we weren't able to help a client was when we were booked to the max, or anytime we were approached by certain specialized industries such as dealerships or other very technically oriented service businesses. While there are only a few industries we can't help, what differentiates us is the fact that we focus on getting these companies someone that can help them regardless of their industry or our knowledge of that particular area.

A strategic and forward-thinking mindset is something all entrepreneurs lean into when attempting to scale their business. Though no easy feat, with ample education, patience, hard work, and the right attitude—anyone can make something great using the online social media platforms and tools available. Remember: There's no "quick fix" or "one-size-fits-all" full-proof method. Success always begins with an opportunity, and it's your choice to either make the most of that opportunity, or let it slip through your fingers.

Chapter Summaries

How Brands Connect with Matt Bertram

The more you share online, the more you will sell.

If you think back to the first chapter, Mindful Brand Linking (MBL) is a term or acronym that I quasi-created to boil down the core components needed for human connection to happen online.

Throughout this book, I have also gathered other examples of how other Influencers, Entrepreneurs, and Small Business Owners have been doing this in their own lives and with their brands and businesses. They have shared their stories and what has worked for them so that you can apply these strategies in your own life to help you get to the next level.

Let their journeys be a testament as well as a knowledge roadmap for what is possible and of what happens when you truly connect with others through social media!

Dale Carnegie famously laid out the principles in 1936 of how to, *"Win Friends & Influence People"*. Fast forward to today, those same theories still work online as people have not changed all that much as you will just need to orient yourself to the new mediums.

Welcome to the Age of the Internet.

How to Build A Memorable Online Brand with Chris Burres

To successfully thrive in our "information age," we have to adapt to the times today. Everyone is online; everyone represents a brand, and everyone is trying to sell you *something*. Whether it's their life-changing hair care regime, fitness aesthetic, or coaching sessions—everyone is marketing something online. For this reason, Chris emphasizes how crucial it is to create a powerful and compelling voice online. For some, this involves a steep learning curve and lots of time mastering a particular platform; for others, this means to bring your brand from outside the shadows and into plain daylight for everyone to see.

Chris shares multiple marketing strategies and tactics guaranteed to help grow your business in 2020, such as:

1. Develop a unique selling proposition (USP) for your business
2. Become the "Bose Stereo" of the industry—aka HIGH value & never goes on sale.
3. Establish consistent brand messaging.

4. Demonstrate high levels of integrity.

5. Define and use your brand voice.

6. Create a call to action.

7. Conduct competitive research.

8. Partner with an internet marketing company.

9. and Value continual learning.

Overall, Chris's marketing tactics help you successfully scale your business and grow with the changing times online. Once you identify your company brand's USP—a different one, has a clear; yet powerful voice, has a high market value, consistent messaging, and built on integrity. After that, all that's left to do is share it with the world online.

The Secrets of Selling with Billy Bray

In his chapter, "The Secrets of Selling," Billy teaches aspiring entrepreneurs his top 'keys to business success.' Billy lives and runs his business by the mantra: the more you serve others, the more you will, in turn, be served. He encourages his readers to ask how they can help others, rather than asking: what's in it for me? As an entrepreneur himself, Billy says that every entrepreneur is tasked with the role of the "problem solver." He then prompts you to take inventory and dig deep into whether there is a problem that continues to remain unresolved that you believe you can fix. He shares his solution for those facing difficulties solving puzzling moral/ethical issues: The Rotary 4 Way Test. This 24-word code of ethics helps employees and business owners walk in the line of truth:

1. Is it the TRUTH?
2. Is it fair to all concerned?
3. Will it build GOODWILL & BETTER FRIENDSHIPS?
4. Will it be BENEFICIAL to all concerned?

Billy also taught us that the best sales situations are those that are valuable and rare. If your product/service has the perfect trifecta of being valuable, rare, and in-demand — customers will come knocking at your door. Remember, the more scarce a resource, the more valuable it holds to the public, increasing its demand. So, start by offering a unique sales situation that's hard to refuse. This is where your chosen product market comes into play. Where there is a vast market, high demand is sure to coincide. Knowing this, take a second to review what you have to offer and assess whether it meets the high requirements necessary to compete in your chosen niche market.

To effectively maximize the power of strategic selling of your product/service to the masses, Billy recommends entering into each sales situation with equal yet high levels of conviction and persuasion as both lead to increased sales.

As you may remember, Billy overcame his fear of selling by repeatedly confronting situations he feared head-on. In doing so, Billy quickly gained the courage, strength, and confidence he needed to become the persuasive salesman he is today. Fear is a human emotion that everyone battles on their journey toward success, and only the top 1% choose courage over fear because what's the other option? Where would you be today if you let fear dictate your life? Likely, not at the top of the business dominance hierarchy.

Lastly, Billy advises us to stop caring so much about what everyone thinks about you because it will hold you back and leave you frozen in fear. Find a valuable, rare, in-demand resource to sell, and take bold action. Move courageously into the unknown one step at a time.

Your Network Determines Your Net Worth with Nolen Davis

There's a great quote that says, "show me your five closest friends, and I'll show you your future." Back in the day, the circle around you to choose from was limited to your general vicinity — perhaps neighbors, classmates, or friends of friends. Through the convent of social media, the pool of friends, mentors, and business associates to pick from is endless.

In his chapter, Nolen shows you how to maximize your online network in various ways. He does so because he has first-hand experience of the value to gain from having an abundant online network at your disposal when marketing a brand. Nolen knows that there is strength in numbers. Sharing your brand message through multiple platforms including but not limited to Facebook, Twitter, Linkedin, and most recently, TikTok will increase brand awareness and engagement tenfold.

Nolen's chapter is for anyone who's wondered: How do I magnify my brand voice and tell the story of my business at the same time?

The answer is simple—by utilizing the power of social media. In particular, Nolen is an advocate of face-to-face live interviews for a live audience. During these interviews, he showcases his service to the audience and allows his customers to share their positive testimonies simultaneously. This bodes well for Nolen's company for multiple reasons.

1. Video content increases audience engagement and organic sales.

2. Live, in-person testimonials bolster believability and authenticity.

3. When you upload a video online, others can share it with friends, family, and colleagues.

Nolen also advises current or aspiring entrepreneurs looking to grow their business to strategically offer a free service, such as a free consultation, for example. This builds customer trust and heightens your brand's integrity.

In summation, Nolen is a visionary. He likes to view his ideas as the 'heavyweight champions' of the world and encourages you to do the same. After all, if you don't believe if what you're selling, why should anyone else? Nolen's takeaway advice for those looking to inspire and lead a successful team is to:

- Love & give freely
- Treat others with respect
- Value passion over money
- Stay true to yourself.

Nolen's goal with this chapter is to inspire you to go all-in on your dreams, inspire greatness, and lead by example, every step of the way.

How to Create a Digital Footprint in the Mortgage industry with Mortgage Mack

As a successful mortgage professional for over 25 years, Mack teaches you how to make a break in the mortgage industry, provides sound advice for aspiring entrepreneurs, and how you can thrive in the digital age of social media. Mack delves into his career as a mortgage professional and shares what he believes led to his success in the industry. Above all, Mack made sure to educate and prepare his clients for the seamless process. To achieve this, he recommends adopting a one-on-one coaching method for a more personal, direct business approach.

Through consistency and long-term success as a mortgage professional, Mack soon became known as the expert, or as we have learned throughout this book, "Trusted Advisor" in his specialty, construction loans. In fact, through one quick google search of "MortgageMack," you will find he has over 30 five-star reviews on the front pages of google. Mack's online presence is an example for aspiring entrepreneurs. It should be a goal that every time a potential or current customer of yours googles your name or business — immediately they're flooded with hundreds of positive reviews and helpful information about your product/service. This builds tremendous trust, credibility, and authority — all of which lead to more sales, revenue, and brand exposure.

Mack gives a few helpful tips for aspiring entrepreneurs, such as:

- Be solution-oriented
- Leverage Personal Relationships
- Utilize Podcasts in 2020 to Grow your Brand Presence
- Never Underestimate the Power of Word-of-Mouth & Referrals
- And lastly, find a Mentor.

On a final note, Matt encourages you to broaden your sphere of influence through Facebook live, Instagram, Linkedin, Email Marketing, Podcasts, and so much more. He recommends capitalizing on the ability to connect with thousands of like-minded business professionals all across the world.

Build a Strong Foundation for Your Business with Randall Chesnutt

Ultimately, every entrepreneur wants their business to be "Spoken About." In his chapter, "Build a Strong Foundation for Your Business," Randall explores what separates the average businessperson from the 'outliers'—the tiger from the sheep—the ordinary from the *extra*ordinary.

He starts by identifying the *Who, What, and Why* of your company/product/service.

- Who are you going to serve?
- What are you going to offer them?

- Why should they choose you over all the competition?

For Randall, the first step in making your business "Spoken About," is to craft a message worth hearing on social media. This is where the help of a marketing agency comes in. But, for those who want to market on their own, Randall has plenty of strategic methods. Here are a few main ones:

1. **The PQAS (problem, question, answer, solution) acronym.** This acronym helps you to pinpoint your target audience's problem and guides you to the solution that creates value.

2. **Create a Clear CTA (Call to Action).** When a potential customer finds your website, the CTA should tell them what to do next (i.e., call x number, set up a free consultation, or request a quote). In the world we live in today, everyone is moving fast—which means everyone wants answers quickly. All your customer wants to know when then find your website is: Can they solve my problem? If not, on to the next.

3. **Address Client Fears Using the "Aha Moment"** The "Aha Moment" is when your customer suddenly realizes the problems preventing them from reaching success within their own business.

4. **Provide an Easy-to-Understand Solution to Your Customers Problems**

    When it comes to problems, everyone's looking for the quickest solution that will cause them the least amount of trouble. In a similar respect, your business/product/service should clearly outline *how easy* it solves your customer's problems *and why*. Randall used Apple's iPod as an example. Apple perfected this strategy in one short sentence, "1,000 CD-quality songs that fit in your pocket."

5. **The PCAN Method for Employee's Intruding Questions/Problems**

PROBLEM: Employee comes into the office to tell me their question.

CAUSE: Determine on your own what is the cause of the problem. Then tell the employee your interpretation.

ANSWER: Ask the employee to tell me what they think the solution to their problem is. If they don't know, ask them to figure it out and come back once they're prepared.

NET-BENEFIT: How do we, the company, and the consumer benefit in the process?

In doing so, before an employee comes to the office with a problem, they will have already thought out its cause, solution, and company benefits from solving said problem.

Lastly, Randall believes strongly in the idea that the early bird gets the worm. He concludes, "Good things come to those who wait. And it's only the things leftover from the people who got there before you."

So, what are you waiting for?

Healthy Body, Healthy Mind with Kailee Wong

Former NFL football player turned business owner tells his story about how he quit the NFL to pursue his dream as an entrepreneur and the lessons he learned along the way. Kailee believes that we're born; we're all built for greatness. He also believes that we're all athletes when we're born. Only as we grow older and life takes its toll our bodies pay the price. While in the NFL, he experienced multiple injuries — thwarting his ability to do his best. Over time, as his pain increased, he decided to quit the NFL to be a better father and to join corporate America.

Soon, Kailee found himself working at non-other than Wall Street. He had a great job with great pay, and everything looked great on paper. That wasn't the case, however. The more Kailee worked, the more bodily pain he experienced. Confused and curious, he asked his co-workers if the experience was mutual? To his surprise, almost everyone admitted experiencing mid-high levels of pain — particularly in the back region. The pain became so unbearable that Kailee could no longer sit for his family dinners. It was then he knew he had to make a drastic change — if not for him, for his family. He then realized that without your health, you have no wealth.

He went all-in towards his dream from that moment forward and opened The Athletic Room in Houston, TX. Kailee wanted to create a place for athletes of all shapes, skills and sizes to meet all their bodily needs. Acupuncture, massage, cold therapy, heat therapy, and more were available in one place at The Athletic Room.

Throughout his chapter Kailee covers six key ways to care for your health:

1. Prioritize recovery
2. Listen to your body
3. Eat healthy to counteract inflammation
4. Improve flexibility & mobility
5. Don't become sedentary
6. Lift weights.

Kailee not only teaches you how to keep your mind and body sharp. He also shares insight into how to make a name for your business on social media in 2020. The main takeaways were to post consistently and to share stories worth hearing online.

How to Turn Adversity into Success with The LinkedIn Authority with Freddy Goerges

More commonly known as the "Linkedin Authority," Freddy Goerges shares how he overcame a difficult time in his life and used his pain as a catalyst for success. In the throes of a divorce and amid financial turmoil, Freddy was at a low spot. He didn't like his job, and he was struggling to make ends meet when his income dropped nearly half. It wasn't until his boss asked him to find HR and business managers for a sale that Freddy decided to create a LinkedIn group. In just under a year, the groups already hit over 1,000 followers, and he received a 20% raise. From that moment forward, his LinkedIn obsession began.

With no wife and little friends, he spent all his time learning everything there is to know about LinkedIn. Freddy would stay up all night sending connections...hoping to create a support network to help him get through the trenches. Moral of the story: In an attempt to escape the looming cloud of darkness, Freddy started to connect with thousands of people on LinkedIn and built a network. In time, people began to see Freddy as an 'Influencer' on the platform—as a leader.

Now, the Linkedin group, Houston Networking Professionals, sits as the largest networking organization on LinkedIn. Freddy's hope in writing this chapter is to motivate aspiring entrepreneurs going through a hard time to use their pain as a drive. Spend all that time alone; you would spend sulking, and pour it into your career, business, goals, etc. Most importantly, whether it's at church, online, chat forums, family, or friends—find a community. Loneliness is the enemy's playground, and isolated people are weak. Even if your support network in your immediate distance is lacking, there are thousands of people all across the globe willing to share a sense of community with you. All you have to do is connect.

Create Shock Value and Prove Your Naysayers Wrong with Taylor Waidhofer

Upon dropping out of university, Taylor started his first entrepreneurial business venture called CluchCity Gifts, a corporate gifting business in the real estate industry. ClutchCity Gifts introduced Taylor into the real estate community and gave him the information necessary to start his business he runs today called Houston Real Producers. Taylor fully utilized social media marketing as a tool to promote his business and pitch his company in front of a group of agents like RE/MAX Paul Baker, and Telebanker. Through this, he caught the eye of some of the top real estate agents in the Houston area as well as built a substantial following on Facebook.

Over time, Taylor leveraged email marketing, Facebook posts, and video content. Now, it hosts the popular podcast, Disruption Nation—interviewing people in the industry 'disrupting' their space in a positive way. Through his experience selling and using social media marketing strategies, Taylor has come up with a few essential pointers to help you launch or grow your business. Here are a few important tips:

1. Find a mentor
2. There are no shortcuts
3. Figure out what success means to you
4. Be a visionary, hire implementers
5. Be better than your naysayers

Today, Taylor is the owner and publisher of Houston Real Producers Magazine and Disruption Nation and hosts monthly educational events with panels exclusively for the staff agents and advertising partners in the city that fund his business. To date, Taylor has partnered with over 75 of the best companies. His audience closed a minimum of $17 million last year, which led to over 25,000 transactions and over 10 million dollars in closed business

Acknowledgements & Works Cited

How Brands Connect with Matt Bertram

Bio

Matt Bertram, local keynote speaker, personal brand consultant, and author of the Amazon Best Seller *Build Your Brand Mania: How to Transform Yourself Into an Authoritative Brand That Will Attract Your Ideal Customers*, is the co-owner and majority shareholder of EWR Digital, a leading digital marketing agency based out of Houston.

Under Matt's leadership, the full-service digital agency has garnered 122, 5-star reviews on Google and grown by 400%. Since launching in 1999, EWR Digital, formerly known as eWebResults, has been internationally recognized as a leading company in SEO and earned media for the SMB market. He currently manages over $10 million in advertising dollars for top clientele across various verticals and geographies world wide from the local home service provider to Fortune 500 companies. He has also mentored multiple funded startups across the US. Bertram also has a robust digital strategy consultancy and has been a guest on over 50 podcasts and quoted in numerous articles published by Forbes, Convert Kit, CyberCoders, Search Engine Journal, Houston Real Producers, and more.

Besides his EWR Digital duties, Matt co-hosts two well-received podcasts, "Houston Business Podcast, presented by the BBB, and the "SEO Podcast: The Unknown Secrets of Internet Marketing" with EWR Digital co-founder Chris Burres. To date, the podcast has over 4 million downloads with more than 55,000 monthly loyal listeners and has been recognized as the most popular SEO podcast on iTunes and Ahrefs.

As a digital marketing strategist, Matt has spoken at conferences such as Podfest and participated in successful

Guinness Book of World Record attempts. He has led online marketing programs in agency growth, sales funnels, SEO, and social media marketing. He's an Agency Partner with Google and is an avid lover of everything marketing.

https://www.linkedin.com/in/mattbertramlive/
https://www.ewrdigital.com/

Sources:

- https://www.asurion.com/about/press-releases/americans-dont-want-to-unplug-from-phones-while-on-vacation-de "https://www.asurion.com/about/press-releases/americans-dont-want-to-unplug-from-phones-while-on-vacation-despite-latest-digital-detox-trend/"spite-latest-digital-detox-trend/
- https://www.socialmediatoday.com/news/how-much-data-is-generated-every-minute-infographic-1/525692/
- https://www.lucidpress.com/blog/how-to-create-brand-voice
- https://static.googleusercontent.com/media/guidelines.raterhub.com/en//searchqualityevaluatorguidelines.pdf
- https://sproutsocial.com/insights/data/social-media-connec HYPERLINK "https://sproutsocial.com/insights/data/social-media-connection/"tion/

- https://www.brandingstrategyinsider.com/linking-brand-essence-and-growth/#.Xp9uvshKhPY
- https://www.cbinsights.com/research/what-is-psychographics/

How to Build A Memorable Online Brand with Chris Burres

Bio

Chris Burres is a research engineer and scientist whose primary mission is to help people live longer, healthier, pain-free lives. Burres has a diverse background in the field of inventions, manufacturing, and internet technology. With a BS in Mechanical Engineering (Minors in Computer Science and Math) from University of Houston, Burres is a co-inventor of patents related to the use of explosives in downhole oil well drilling, a co-inventor of the most efficient fullerene manufacturing equipment in use since 1991, and co-owner of a company that manufactures a unique product containing a Nobel-Prize winning molecule that has been shown to extend the lifespan of test subjects by 90 percent.

In 1991, Burres co-founded SES Research, the first company to deliver commercial quantities of Carbon Nanomaterials. In 2012, his company provided the raw ingredient, ESS60 to a group of researchers, which ultimately led to the longest longevity experiment known to man. In the now famous study, referred to as the "2012 Paris Baati Study," the test subjects, rats, lived 90 percent longer than the control group, and unlike the control group, none of them died with tumors. This Nobel-Prize winning molecule began to quickly produce tens of thousands of testimonials from users and inspired Burres to fulfill his mission to help others to live pain-free, healthy lives, or as he likes to say, Live Beyond the Norms. He has made a conscious choice to increase awareness of this product throughout the United States and beyond. In an effort to expand the knowledge around his company, he is currently working with Oura Ring, and they are jointly conducting studies to verify the positive impact the MyVitalC formulation has on sleep as already reported by many of the formulation users.

Burres's interest in health as well as safety extends to technology – he co-wrote the health care app that Harvard medical school declared to be the most accurate online symptom checker available, and he wrote the software program for a manufacturing plant that provides a solution to the aging 2.4 million miles of pipeline which is rapidly approaching its viable lifespan and poses severe threats to our safety.

Burres is a charismatic and engaging presenter and speaker; he is the co-host of the most popular SEO podcast on iTunes with over 4 million downloads since 2009, and he performed onstage as a professional improv artist for 5 years entertaining audiences weekly at Third Coast Comedy in Houston, Texas. He has also been playing soccer for over 25 years; he played semi-professional soccer and was the Player/Coach for the University of Houston Soccer team.

Burres is also co-founder of eWebResults now EWR Digital, one of the largest digital marketing agencies in the 4th largest city in the US: Houston, Texas.

https://www.myvitalc.com/

https://www.ewrdigital.com/

https://www.linkedin.com/in/chrisburres/

The Secrets of Selling with Billy Bray

Bio:

https://www.linkedin.com/in/billybray/

https://www.outsourcedrm.com/

Sources:

https://www.directory-online.com/Rotary/Accounts/7475/Downloads/5556/rotary%20fourway%20test.pdf

The Benefits of Social Media Networking with Nolen Davis

Bio:

- https://www.upsocialnetwork.com/
- https://www.vidsinc.com/
- https://www.nolendavis.com
- https://www.linkedin.com/in/nolendavis/

How to Create a Digital Footprint in the Mortgage industry with Mortgage Mack

Bio:

- **Website:** http://teammortgagemack.com/
- **Linkedin:** https://www.linkedin.com/in/mortgagemack/
- **Facebook Live:** https://www.facebook.com/mortgeagemack/

Build a Strong Foundation for Your Business with Randall Chesnutt

Bio

https://www.linkedin.com/in/socialmediarandall/

www.RandallChesnutt.com

Sources:

- https://www.lifewire.com/who-invented-the-ipod-2000700

- https://www.macworld.com/article/1163181/the-birth-of-the-ipod.html
- https://www.creative.com/corporate/milestones/?year=1996%20-%202000
- https://medium.com/@chep2m/creative-nomad-vs-ipod-a-case-study-f008b4d9bc40
- https://www.rottentomatoes.com/m/good_will_hunting/quotes/
- https://www.cnbc.com/2017/09/20/how-mypillow-founder-went-from-crack-addict-to-self-made-millionaire.html
- https://www.youtube.com/watch?v=3FqPmkq7_Ek

Healthy Body, Healthy Mind with Kailee Wong

Bio

https://www.linkedin.com/in/kailee-wong-5b414910/

https://theathleticroom.com/

Sources:

- https://www.ncbi.nlm.nih.gov/pmc/articles/PMC4934575/
- https://uk.reuters.com/article/health-testosterone-levels-dc-idUKKIM16976320061101
- https://pediatrics.aappublications.org/content/131/1/183

How to Turn Adversity into Success with The LinkedIn Authority with Freddy Goerges

Bio

https://www.linkedin.com/in/freddygoerges/
https://houstonyoungprofessionals.com/

Create Shock Value and Prove Your Naysayers Wrong with Taylor Waidhofer

Bio

Taylor Waidhofer is the Owner and Publisher of Houston Real Producers, a trade magazine for the top 500 Realtors in the Houston market. Established in 2017, Houston Real Producers has been helping local real estate agents connect with top businesses across Houston.

He also is the host of a podcast and YouTube channel show, "Disruption Nation" and also host events and educational events with panels and keynote speakers to add value to the real estate community called Masterclass Houston. He's also a proud father to 2 sons and enjoys spending his free time fishing with his family on weekends.

- YouTube channel: https://www.youtube.com/channel/UCpOX4EWyXcy30wun1wtF3nA
- HRP FB page: https://www.facebook.com/houstonrealproducers/
- Personal FB: https://www.facebook.com/taywaidhofer
- LinkedIn: https://www.linkedin.com/in/taywaidhofer/
- Instagram: https://www.instagram.com/taywaidhofer/
- Twitter: https://twitter.com/taywaidhofer
- Podcast: https://anchor.fm/disruptionnation/
- Website: http://houstonrealproducers.com/
- Eventbrite: http://masterclasshouston.com/

Growth Strategies to Scale your Business in the Digital Era with Sami Khaleeq

Bio

Before Sami Khaleeq made his break into digital marketing, he worked in cybersecurity. At this job, he learned to prioritize patience and education more than anything else in the business. Sami then launched CG Studio, a branding and digital marketing strategy consulting firm/agency where he builds and implements strategies for his clients. By implementing marketing strategies, he helps his clients scale their business and improve their brand visibility online.

Throughout his time working as an entrepreneur, Sami has gained valuable knowledge that he shares in the chapter. His top five forward-thinking tips for growing your business online are as follows:

1. Create a multi-channel presence
2. Value client trust over a cheap sale
3. Education. Education. Education
4. Value attitude over skill-set
5. There is no "quick-fix" to grow your business overnight

Ultimately, developing a strategic and forward-thinking mindset doesn't happen in the blink of an eye. It takes patience, education, grit, and above all else, a belief in yourself.

- https://www.linkedin.com/in/samikhaleeq/
- https://cgsdigitalmarketing.com/about/

Other Acknowledgements

Corrine Moore - Corresponding Author
Jennifer Ramirez - Editor

www.ingramcontent.com/pod-product-compliance
Lightning Source LLC
Chambersburg PA
CBHW031629210526
45464CB00004B/1816